MANAGING STRATEGY

David Watson

Open University Press
Buckingham · Philadelphia

Open University Press
Celtic Court
22 Ballmoor
Buckingham
MK18 1XW

e-mail: equiries@openup.co.uk
world wide web: http://www.openup.co.uk

and
325 Chestnut Street
Philadelphia, PA 19106, USA

First published 2000

A catalogue record of this book is available from the British Library

ISBN   0 335 20345 0 (pb)   0 335 20346 9 (hb)

Library of Congress Cataloging-in-Publication Data
Watson, David, 1949–
    Managing strategy / by David Watson.
        p.   cm. – (Managing universities and colleges)
    Includes bibliographical references (p.   ) and index.
    ISBN 0–335–20345–0 (pbk.). – ISBN 0–335–20346–9 (hard)
    1. Universities and colleges–Great Britain–Administration.
2. Strategic planning–Great Britain.   3. Education, Higher–Great
Britain–Management.   I. Title.   II. Series.
LB2341.8.G7W28   2000
378.41–dc21   99–44707
                                                                CIP

Typeset by Graphicraft Limited, Hong Kong
Printed in Great Britain by The Cromwell Press, Trowbridge

For Betty Pinto Skolnick

CONTENTS

FOREWORD

Lord Ron Dearing, Chairman of the National
Committee of Inquiry into Higher Education

In our Committee's report, *Higher Education in the Learning Society*, presented to the UK government in 1997, we were in no doubt about the established role of higher education in ensuring the social, cultural and economic wellbeing of our nation. Equally, we were deeply conscious of how higher education institutions were under new and increasing pressure as we approached the Millennium, and how they would have to continue to change and develop to sustain their distinctive contribution to individuals and society. The solution to the twin demands – of continuity and change – we saw encapsulated in the concept of a 'new compact' between the institutions, individually and collectively, society and the state. In the first chapter we attempted to outline the evolving relationship, as follows.

> At the heart of our vision of higher education is the free-standing institution, which offers teaching to the highest level in an environment of scholarship and independent enquiry. But, collectively and individually, these institutions are becoming ever more central to the economic wellbeing of the nation, localities and individuals. There is a growing bond of interdependence, in which each is looking for much from the other. That interdependence needs to be more clearly recognised by all the participants.
> (NCIHE 1997: 11)

From the institutional perspective, responding to this challenge places an ever-increasing premium on the capacity of the college or university to understand and manage its strategic direction. To some, such a statement may appear philistine or insensitive to the historical image of the academy as a place apart from the rest of society, and certainly from the economy. It may also be seen as a disguised attack on the independence of both the institutions and the academics who work within them. To the Committee, and the vast majority of those who contributed to our endeavours through written and oral submissions, as well as in creative, sometimes passionate, dialogue, such arguments are anachronistic and misleading. They misunderstand not only the honourable traditions of higher education in assessment and critique of society and culture but also its decisive role in creating and ensuring the application of the knowledge that enables us to go forward. 'Managing strategy' is a constructive and creative, if not to say a vital element of the independence as well as of the effectiveness of a college or university.

As one of the 'institutional' members of the Committee, David Watson contributed directly to our understanding of higher education strategy from an institutional point of view. In his book he defends not only the proposition for continuity in a climate of change, but also the need for rational analysis and careful planning of an individual institution's contribution to the development of a national sector of higher education that is admired (and imitated) around the world.

SERIES EDITORS' INTRODUCTION

Post-secondary educational institutions can be viewed from a variety of different perspectives. For most of the students and staff who work in them, they are centres of learning and teaching where the participants are there by choice and consequently, by and large, work very hard. Research has always been important in some higher education institutions (HEIs), but in recent years this emphasis has grown and what for many was a great pleasure and, indeed, a treat, is becoming more of a threat and an insatiable performance indicator that just has to be met. Maintaining the correct balance between quality research and learning/teaching, while the unit of resource continues to decline inexorably, is one of the key issues facing us all. Educational institutions as work places must be positive and not negative environments.

From another aspect, post-secondary educational institutions are clearly communities, functioning to all intents and purposes like small towns and internally requiring and providing a similar range of services, while also having very specialist needs. From yet another they are seen as external suppliers of services to industry, commerce and the professions. These 'customers' receive, *inter alia*, a continuing flow of well qualified fresh graduates with transferable skills; part-time and short course study opportunities through which to develop existing employees; consultancy services to solve problems and help expand business; and research and development support to create new breakthroughs.

However, educational institutions are also significant businesses in their own right. One recent study of the economic impact of higher education in Wales shows that it is of similar importance in employment terms to the steel or banking/finance sectors. Put another way, Welsh HEIs spend half a billion pounds annually and create more than 23,000 full-time equivalent jobs. And it must be remembered that there are only 13 HEIs in Wales, compared with 171 in the whole of the UK, and that these Welsh institutions are, on average, relatively small. In addition, it has recently been realized that UK higher education is a major export industry with the added benefit of long-term financial and political returns. If the UK further education sector is also added to this equation, the economic impact of post-secondary education is of truly startling proportions.

Whatever perspective you take, it is obvious that educational institutions require managing and, consequently, this series has been produced to facilitate that end. The editors have striven to identify authors who are distinguished practitioners in their own right and, indeed, can also write. The authors have been given the challenge of producing essentially practical handbooks that combine appropriate theory and contextual material with examples of good practice and guidance where appropriate.

The topics chosen are both of key importance to educational management and stand at the forefront of current debate. Some of these topics have never been covered in depth before and all of them are equally applicable to further as well as higher education. The editors are firmly of the belief that the UK distinction between these sectors will continue to blur and will be replaced, as in many other countries, by a continuum where the management issues are entirely common.

For well over a decade, both of the editors have been involved with a management development programme for senior staff from HEIs throughout the world. Every year the participants quickly learn that we share the same problems and that similar solutions are normally applicable. Political and cultural differences may on occasion be important, but are often no more than an overlying veneer. Hence, this series will be of considerable relevance and value to post-secondary educational managers in many countries.

For a similar period of time, both of the editors have also jointly directed the Committee of Vice-Chancellors and Principals' (CVCP) annual development programme for 'rising' UK administrators. This week-long programme operates on a matrix basis, involving a series of regular inputs from distinguished senior administrators and academics, while the participants simultaneously work in separate teams to prepare strategic plans for four hypothetical universities. At the end of the course these plans are presented to, and judged by, mock Funding Council assessors. Consequently, the editors are fully aware, in both their own working and teaching lives, of the importance, difficulties and frustrations of educational strategic planning.

This volume is, therefore, of particular significance. It has been written by a senior vice-chancellor, recently knighted for his services to higher education, who has worked in a range of institutions and was a member of the Dearing Committee. David Watson has produced a work that reveals a masterly grasp of the subject and an awesome knowledge of the contemporary literature. He has been forgiven by the editors for his more reflective approach than the norm for this series, because the gains far outweigh the losses. In any case, the lengthy Appendix, which comprises a fully worked example of a University Corporate Plan, provides much practical guidance and food for thought. This is an important work.

David Warner
David Palfreyman

PREFACE AND ACKNOWLEDGEMENTS

Despite the fact that it appears in a highly practical series, this book is deliberately not an operational handbook. The literature on strategic management abounds in these, and readers seeking detailed manuals on how to set up spreadsheets, Gantt charts and flow diagrams structured around the hierarchy of missions, aims and objectives (and, perhaps more importantly, identifying who is responsible for their delivery, and by when), should go straight to the bibliography and pick up some signposts from there (see, for example, Bowman and Asch 1996: 110–11; Thomas 1996: 45; Bruce 1999). There is a particularly good introductory workbook published by the Office for Public Management (Tarplett and Parston 1998). In contrast, for a personal odyssey through the major issues, along with a description of maps and tools employed, I recommend Phil Meade's account of the strategic re-orientation of the University of Otago (Meade 1997). In 2000 the English Funding Council will produce their own guide, *Strategic Planning in the HE Sector*, with a valuable set of 'self-challenge questions' (HEFCE forthcoming).

This is more of a reflective essay on what strategic management can and should consist of in a modern, essentially democratic university or college environment, and how to make it work. For the book to be genuinely a guide to good practice, I contend that these issues need to be fully understood and a set of contributory values absorbed.

As a consequence, I take a somewhat different line on the question of university 'culture' than most of the current literature. The latter divides fairly neatly into two camps: defenders of an imagined golden age of university autonomy (and isolation) *versus* advocates of a new 'managerial' approach to questions of efficiency, effectiveness and customer satisfaction. The former spend most of their time regretting the approach of the latter, and vice versa. The tone is frequently unscholarly and sometimes even violent.

The approach taken here is different. The academy has to change, not least to meet the needs of a rapidly changing host society as well as a more diverse, plural and democratic internal community. But it also has to cling on to some bedrock convictions about what higher education *is* and, even more emphatically, what it is *for*. This presupposes a strategic and management philosophy that is simultaneously careful of traditional values, restorative of those that have fallen into abeyance (or possibly never lived up to the full range of what they claimed) and innovative (to the point of revolution if necessary) in the genuine interests of that society and that special community.

The relatively recent emergence of an academic and professional genre called 'higher education management' has both hindered and helped this understanding. On the one hand it has brought disciplined insight into the operational problems and possibilities of highly complex organizations, torn one way by their need to compete and survive in a market-place and another by their need to maintain dignity and independence (and a degree of other-worldliness) as a critical public service. Thus it has been generally helpful for universities and colleges to be encouraged to face up to modern standards of personnel, financial and other corporate practice. On the other hand a discourse about 'management' has from time to time been captured either by 'managers' insensitive to the special history and conditions of higher education or by the 'managed', who either fail to recognize, let alone accept, the 'real-world' situation of their employers or who engage in proxy battles with managers in support of causes over which the latter may have little real control. Thus the prophets of 'management of change' face up to those more interested in 'change of management'.

Methodologically the genre has yet to find its feet. It has a restricted set of styles of analysis – soft ethnography meets the Harvard Business School – and its own vocabulary (which often seems designed to antagonize the theorists of traditional academic life). Contested concepts include (for managers), 'leadership' (and its exhaustive typologies) or 'changing the culture'. This is challenged by defensive re-grouping (by the managed) around 'autonomy', 'academic freedom' or the critique of 'new managerialism'. Whether or not what follows successfully avoids this Manichean tendency only the reader can judge.

As will be soon apparent, the majority of the case study material on which the book depends is drawn from my own experience of the development of the English higher education system over the past quarter century. I have, however, tried to draw upon the parallel trajectories of the other parts of the United Kingdom as well as the contemporary literature about developments in North America, Australasia and continental Europe.

Having emphasized the personal quality of this endeavour, it is also important to indemnify as far as possible those from whom I have learned and those by whom I have been inspired in the often paradoxical task of trying to 'manage' academic enterprises. Thus, while absolving them unconditionally from responsibility for what follows, I would like to thank the late Lord Eric Ashby, Professor Geoff Doherty and Lord Ron Dearing, as well as colleagues and former colleagues at Crewe & Alsager College, Oxford Polytechnic and the University of Brighton. Comments on an early draft from David House and Stuart Laing in particular caused me to think again. Ruth Farwell (now of South Bank University) was an important co-conspirator in the production of the material in the Appendix. Also extremely helpful were John Skelton of the Open University Press, David Warner, co-editor of the series, and Rachel Bowden of the Education Research Centre at the University of Brighton, who gave professional, practical and moral support every step of the tortuous path of producing the book. Finally, Betty Skolnick, Sarah Watson and Michael Watson performed their usual invaluable task of reminding me that there are more important things in life than the future of higher education.

ACRONYMS AND ABBREVIATIONS

ABRC	Advisory Board for the Research Councils
ACL	Action-Centred Leadership
AGR	Association of Graduate Recruiters
AHUA	Association of Heads of University Administration
AUCC	Association for University and College Counselling
BECTA	British Educational Communications and Technology Agency
BUFDG	British Universities Finance Directors Group
CAT	College of Advanced Technology
CATS	Credit Accumulation and Transfer Scheme
CBI	Confederation of British Industry
CENTRIM	Centre for Research in Innovation Management
CEO	chief executive officer
CIHE	Council for Industry and Higher Education
CIPFA	Chartered Institute of Public Finance and Accountancy
CNAA	Council for National Academic Awards
COPS	Complex Product Systems (Innovation Centre)
COSHEP	Committee of Scottish Higher Education Principals
CPD	continuing professional development
CSR	Comprehensive Spending Review
CRE	Commission for Racial Equality
CUC	Committee of University Chairmen
CUCO	Commission on University Career Opportunity
CVCP	Committee of Vice-Chancellors and Principals
CVE	continuing vocational education
DENI	Department of Education Northern Ireland
DES	Department of Education and Science

DETR	Department of the Environment, Transport and the Regions
DfEE	Department for Education and Employment
DoE	Department of the Environment
EC	European Commission
ECS	Education Counselling Service
EOC	Equal Opportunities Commission
ESRC	Economic and Social Research Council
EU	European Union
FCs	Funding Councils
FEFC	Further Education Funding Council
FTE	full-time equivalent
GOSE	Government Office for the South East
HERDF	Higher Education Regional Development Fund
HESA	Higher Education Statistics Agency
HEFCE	Higher Education Funding Council for England
HEFCW	Higher Education Funding Council for Wales
HEIs	higher education institutions
HEQC	Higher Education Quality Council
HEQE	Higher education: quality and employability
HSE	Health and Safety Executive
ICT	information and communication technologies
IIP	Investors in People
IiYP	Investing in Young People
ILAs	Individual Learning Accounts
ILT	Institute for Learning and Teaching
INSET	in-service education of teachers
IOD	Institute of Directors
IPR	intellectual property rights
IT	information technology
ITRI	Information Technology Research Institute
JCPSG	Joint Costing and Pricing Steering Group
JISC	Joint Information Systems Committee
JPPSG	Joint Procurement Policy and Strategy Group
JSA	Jobseekers' Allowance
LEA	Local Education Authority
LMI	labour market information
MAC	Management and Administrative Computing
MASNs	maximum aggregate student numbers
MSF	Manufacturing, Science and Finance
NATFHE	National Association of Teachers in Further and Higher Education
NAO	National Audit Office
NCIHE	National Committee of Inquiry into Higher Education

NETTs	National Education and Training Targets
NHS	National Health Service
NVQ	National Vocational Qualification
OECD	Organization for Economic Cooperation and Development
OFSTED	Office for Standards in Education
OPCS	Office of Population Censuses and Surveys
PFI	Private Finance Initiative
PISG	Performance Indicators Steering Group
PPP	public–private partnership
PQA	post-qualifications admissions
QA	quality assurance
QAA	Quality Assurance Agency
QAAHE	Quality Assurance Agency for Higher Education
RAE	research assessment exercise
RDAs	Regional Development Agencies
ROAs	Records of Achievement
RSA	Royal Society of Arts
SCOP	Standing Committee of Principals
SEANET	South of England Accreditation Network
SHEFC	Scottish Higher Education Funding Council
SMEs	small and medium-sized enterprises
SORP	Statement of Recommended (Accounting) Practice
SPRU	Science Policy Research Unit
TEC	Training and Enterprise Council
TQA	teaching quality assessment
TTA	Teacher Training Agency
TVU	Thames Valley University
UCEA	Universities and Colleges Employers Association
UFC	Universities Funding Council
UGC	University Grants Committee
UKERNA	United Kingdom Education and Research Networking Association
UNESCO	United Nations Educational, Scientific and Cultural Organization
USA	Universities Safety Association
USS	Universities Superannuation Scheme

FIGURE, TABLES AND APPENDICES

INTRODUCTION: INSIDE THE ACADEMIC COMMUNITY

The question of culture

Managing strategy is arguably the most important thing a college or university does, enabling all of its core activities of teaching, research and wider social and economic service to be optimally achieved. It involves a thorough knowledge of the institution's present strengths and weaknesses and the making of choices about the future. Good analysis and intelligent choices will ensure the exploitation of opportunities, the avoidance of disaster and improved reputational positioning. A sound, well expressed strategy will encapsulate the institution's self-identity, gather business and win friends. Above all it will help to structure the experience and commitment of the people who work for and with the enterprise, giving them a source of personal as well as collective pride.

That, at least, is the theory. The gap between such theory and the practice of managing strategy in higher education institutions, as well as the reasons for it, is highly revealing about the special characteristics of colleges and universities as organizations.

First there is the paradox of autonomous, proudly independent institutions sitting in a sector with a set of collective and mutual commitments and responsibilities. In setting strategic priorities at both institutional and sector level the tensions between competition and collaboration can often become disabling.

Simultaneously, members of the senior management team have to marry a volatile and unpredictable external environment with the internal dynamics and trajectory of their own institution. In the context of strategic statements this can often lead to blandness and inclusiveness where distinctiveness and differentiation should apply. 'Mission statements' thus frequently become lists of unprioritized options on the entirely rational basis of keeping open options that can be strongly influenced by others (for example, near-monopoly purchasers of goods and services) (Watson 1998: 66). Universities and colleges have by no means escaped the lure of the 'universal' mission statement satirized by Guy Browning in his 'Office Politics' column:

> We are committed to being world leaders in our industry. We will do this through delighting our customers by the world-class quality of our products and services. Our people are our greatest asset and we are committed to developing and training them. We respect the environment and are conscious of health and safety in everything we do.
>
> (Browning 1999: 59)

Peter Womack of the University of East Anglia likens the academic manifestation of this type of discourse to that of *1984*: 'Even more comprehensively than they are required to be supportive of the regime in general, the inhabitants of Orwell's dystopia are required to be *positive about things in general*' (Womack 1999: 3, original emphasis).

In the heart of the organization, middle managers have to deal with the consequences of traditionally 'flat' structures that are designed around the principle of management by eventual consensus. Taking the development of the curriculum as an example of the key 'product' of the enterprise, the range of authorized opinions on its design and delivery is almost universally coterminous with the community that delivers and supports it. In these circumstances, delivering strategy can never be a matter of command and control.

Finally, at the academic coalface of teaching, research and related 'service', strategic statements can be regarded along a continuum of negativity from indifference to world-weary cynicism. Here, for example, is 'Prinny' – the anonymous faculty correspondent in the University of Sussex *Bulletin* – musing on strategy and change.

> All around are the clamours *for* change – groups looking into credit, part-time degrees, the facilitation of internal and external transfer, lifelong learning, developing links with partner institutions (quick, wash hands now!), Dearing, Graduate Standards, QAA [Quality Assurance Agency] – our ears ring and buzz with it all. I say we must resist it all. Universities are not about 'change' – they are temples of knowledge tended by middle-aged men in corduroy trousers who understand the laws of the

universe. Universities aren't part of society, reflecting the needs of the population – the sun-splashed ivory towers stand today as they always will. Wilson is devaluing the pound, Bobby Moore is the best defensive player in England and the Kinks are an interesting beat combo – if we close our eyes, it will always be 1967!

(Anon 1998: 3)

At the core of such cynicism is the issue of loyalty. Traditional academics do not regard themselves so much as working *for* a university as working *in* it. Asked for information about identity with various causes, they are likely to express greatest solidarity with the interests of a discipline, a slightly lower sense of fellow feeling with the (academic) members of a department, and only then a glimmer of 'membership' of the college or university. (For a detailed understanding of the disciplinary basis of both loyalty and particular patterns of connection see Becher (1989).)

This is, of course, a value hierarchy that has been assaulted over the past decades from a variety of fronts: from the changing map of knowledge, with its corrosion of disciplinary boundaries; from the emerging interprofessionalism of the academic enterprise – teaching as well as research (as other expertise; that of librarians, computer personnel, technicians and others, becomes increasingly important to the team); and finally from 'management', which seems increasingly important to the business of institutional survival and prosperity.

A code for many of these systems of exchange is that of 'collegiality'. In a recent lament about the state of her discipline (cultural studies), Lauren Berlant of the University of Chicago notes that this is 'an area of professional life for which virtually no faculty member is trained', and describes the resultant dangers:

The strangeness of negotiating the odd intimacy of institutional association with colleagues we know well but barely know; the hierarchies of professorship that mediate, though it's never clear how, the personal relationship among faculty members; the interpersonal effort involved in the daily grind of professorship; the strain of optimistic institution building in this difficult context.

(Berlant 1998: 107–8)

'Optimistic institution building in a difficult context' comes as close to an academic's felt definition of strategic planning as is possible.

Theory and practice

Traditional business theory is very clear about where 'strategic management' sits in the scheme of things. In the words of J.L. Moore:

> whether it is termed general management, business policy, corporate strategy, long-range planning or corporate management, the sector has addressed the same issue: the determination of how an organisation, *in its entirety* [original emphasis], can best be directed in a changing world.
>
> (Moore 1992: xi)

Organizations have overarching *missions*, which are as clear and distinctive as possible. (These are, ideally, singular; the rumour is that the Fuji Corporation's unwritten mission was 'Kill Kodak'.) Beneath these they identify broad *goals* and a *strategic plan* aimed at their attainment. Further down still, and in the engine room of day-to-day management, are operational *aims, objectives* and *detailed plans*, with targets, time scales and unambiguously assigned personal and group responsibilities (Bowman and Asch 1996: 1–3).

There is some doubt, even in the Adam Smithian world of the pure market and the invisible hand, that this hierarchy holds true. Richard Whittington has, for example, identified not only four 'generic approaches to strategy', but also their fundamental inadequacy when faced with the strategic choices that most business enterprises have to make to survive:

> The *Classical* approach, the oldest and still the most influential, relies upon the rational planning methods dominant in the textbooks. Next the *Evolutionary* approach draws upon the fatalistic metaphor of biological evolution, but substitutes the discipline of the market for the law of the jungle. *Processualists* emphasise the sticky imperfect nature of all human life, pragmatically accommodating strategy to the fallible processes of both organisations and markets. Finally, the *Systemic* approach is relativistic, regarding the ends and means of strategy as inescapably linked to the cultures and powers of the local social system in which it takes place.
>
> (Whittington 1993: 2, original emphasis)

Each approach has its own distinctive strengths and weaknesses, but Whittington's clear preference is for the 'systemic'. His reasons will resonate well with the particular demands placed upon higher education, especially the 'belief that strategy reflects the particular social systems in which strategists participate, defining for them the interests in which they act and the rules by which they survive' (Whittington 1993: 5).

As character types, all of Whittington's personalities undoubtedly occur among the senior leaders of colleges and universities, although again the 'systemic' probably dominates among the most effective:

> In the politics of organisational careers and decision-making, the Systemic perspective arms managers with sardonic self-awareness. Getting ahead involves not just merit, but also social conformity . . . Sociologically sensitive and just a little bit cynical, the Systemic manager is just as confident as the Classicist in planning her future. The difference is that she secures her advance by drawing on a much more catholic range of social resources, and manipulates them with far greater sophistication.
> (Whittington 1993: 136)

What this type of analysis misses, however, in the special circumstances of higher education, is the lack of power of managers (individually or in teams) to act upon their instincts without considering (some would say calculating) how to carry along with them the other individuals and groups with whom they share direct responsibility for the quality and the success of the enterprise.

In these circumstances one of the touchstones of the success of the enterprise is the management of morale. In common with most of the public services at the end of the twentieth century, higher education has felt enormous pressure on collective and individual morale, and suffered above average incidence of the impact of low morale (in, for example, extremely high – or extremely low – rates of turnover, and in the rates of stress-related illnesses) (Lacey 1998). The objective causes of such problems are fairly easy to determine, and most can be traced to the effect of underfunded expansion multiplied by increased external scrutiny and accountability. Similarly, critics wishing to lay the cause of increased stress on management practice often ignore the evidence of stressors that start outside the workplace – or those that are, at least in this era, shared by other major employment sectors (such as reduced job security). None the less, morale is a key component of internal culture in higher education, and hence needs to be carefully analysed.

That said, morale is notoriously hard to measure (House and Watson 1995: 8–10). Morale surveys are popular with trade unions, who often see them as preliminary steps towards votes of confidence and changes of management (Tysome 1997; Utley 1998). For identical reasons, they are unpopular with managers. If carried out in a sophisticated way they can, however, often be subtly revealing, showing across the public sector, for example: concerns about pay and other aspects of personal reward falling below those of professional status; client support; growth of bureaucracy; and other aspects of conditions of service such as 'family-friendly' policies on childcare and parental leave (Lindsay 1987; Office of Population Censuses and Surveys (OPCS) 1995: 45–6).

'New' managerialism

It is an easy charge to represent these pressures and a uniform management response to them as new, especially as a response to the rapid expansion of higher education stimulated by the Conservative government from the mid-1980s (Deem 1998a; Trowler 1998a, 1998b).

Rosemary Deem, for example, defines 'new management' as 'a complex ideology that informs ways of managing public institutions by advocating many of the practices and values of the private for-profit sector in pursuit of efficiency, excellence and continuous improvement'. She contrasts it with a softer, more sensitive approach, rooted in 'the uncertainties of late modernity', focusing on 'citizenship and public participation' and the development of 'public service values', summed up as 'new public service managerialism'. She is, however, sceptical about there being any real instances of this being applied successfully in universities. Finally she posits a radical alternative, of 'femocracy', stressing 'collaborative and facilitative management, concern for people rather than just focusing on tasks, a lack of interest in personal status and competing with others, flexibility in approach and . . . ability to work as a member of a team'. Her research indicates empirical examples of such successful applications, although rather more at the departmental than the institutional level.

She does, however, concede that such characteristics may not in fact be gender inspired: an adjustment in at least definitional terms that seems to be given weight by recent research from Cranfield (Deem 1998b; Korac-Kakabadse *et al.* 1998; Trapp 1998). In this study a careful differentiation is made between issues of promotion and career progression ('getting there') and style and effectiveness of performance in senior roles ('being there'). In the former, gender is manifestly a source of discrimination, and a validation of the 'glass ceiling'. However, the 'leadership philosophies' of the most successful managers who *have* arrived connect more directly with variables like age and experience than gender. The study is primarily concerned with data from the UK's National Health Service (NHS) and the Australian Public Service, but its broad conclusions also ring true for higher education (Korac-Kakabadse *et al.* 1998: 382–3).

Paul Trowler takes a different tack. For him, all the ills of the British academic estate at the turn of the twentieth century can be laid at the door of 'management'. In a quasi-ethnographic study of one thinly-disguised institution (more accurately, one course team), resentments, anxieties and a range of professional concerns (especially over the introduction of modularity) are all collapsed into this, no doubt emotionally satisfying, call to arms (Trowler 1998a). Sadly, students and their interests (the other part of this eternal triangle) are conspicuous by their absence. In a later, more general text, Trowler further simplifies his critique. For him, in the 1980s:

> education management became largely viewed as applying a set of tools, derived from management approaches in other contexts, to the task that had been set . . . Ideas and practices based on management in industry began to pervade schools and other institutions, and the discourse of educational management began to change.
>
> (Trowler 1998b: 97–9)

There are various problems with the more simplistic versions of the 'new managerial' charge-sheet. Firstly, while 'management' and 'managers' may sometimes be 'hard', it is naive to call this pathology 'new'. It ignores a long line of baronial deans and heads of departments, as well as eccentric and ruthless heads of institutions. If anything, these individuals have been subject to new and timely discipline as a result of modern developments in governance and accountability. Secondly, 'hard management' is as much a bit of ideologically committed code as any of the other developments whose advent its adherents deplore. The fundamental presupposition is that what has been 'managed' is fundamentally to the detriment of the institutions, their members and the society that has supported them, including such sector-wide priorities as access and expansion. Thirdly, it depends upon a mythological view of institutional history, as powerful as the myth of Anglo-Saxon freedom was for the early English parliamentarians. Principally it centres around the view that universities and colleges operated effectively in the past and would operate effectively today on a basis of management by 'eventual consensus'. As Professor Ted Wragg once joked, 'the prospect of a university Senate trying to decide what to do with a free kick on the edge of the penalty area is too awful to contemplate' (Wragg 1997). Fourthly, it has spawned the entirely new idea that managers and management decisions should be subject to instant and binding democratic recall, as in the cynicism with which some industrial relations practices have developed (like the 'votes of confidence' referred to above).

Finally, there is a strong element of special pleading at play. Despite the slipping of pay parity (this has been true of almost all public sector professionals), and the increase in the proportion of short-term contracts, over the past few decades there has apparently been no problem with renewal of the profession and, with some exceptions (for example the effects of cuts on the then 'university' sector in the early 1980s), no significant down-sizing (Watson and Taylor 1998: 109–14).

To return to the 'question of culture', internal cynicism about 'management' (which may very well be endemic, or at least irreducible beneath a certain level) should not be allowed to overcome or disguise the strengths of the academic community that it is appropriate to affirm, and even to celebrate. It is, for example, reassuring that so many outside still wish to join in. Student demand, despite the demographic and economic gloom-mongers, continues to rise. Industry and commerce, as well as government and the public service, still see universities as the first call for research and the more reflective and long-term aspects of consultancy. Moreover, there is growing evidence that the recent democratization of higher education has broken down barriers between colleges and universities and their 'host' communities, which are now much more likely to look at 'their' institutions in a positive and affectionate light.

International perspectives

As acknowledged at the outset, this book draws upon UK (and predominantly English) experience. It should, however, have distinct international resonance, as so many of the problems (and proposed solutions) of university strategy are currently strongly converging around the world. The United Nations Educational, Scientific and Cultural Organization's (UNESCO) *Draft World Declaration on Higher Education for the Twenty-first Century*, agreed in Paris in October 1998, begins boldly enough:

On the eve of a new century, there is an unprecedented demand for and a great diversification in higher education, as well as an increased awareness of its vital importance for sociocultural and economic development, and for building the future, for which the younger generation will need to be equipped with new skills, knowledge and ideals.

(UNESCO 1998: 1)

In similar terms the 'Glion Colloquium' of North American and European Universities, meeting in May 1998, saw 'a unique and crucial role' for universities and colleges in the new Millennium:

> They are the chief agents of discovery, the major providers of basic research that underlies new technology and improved health care, they are the engines of economic growth, the custodians and transmitters of cultural heritage, the mentors of each new generation of entrants into every profession, the accreditors of competency and skill, the agents of personal understanding and societal transformation. In them, on a daily basis the young and the old seek to bring wisdom, insight and skill to bear in the daunting complexities of human affairs.

(Glion Colloquium 1998: 4)

These bold claims require some historical and comparative analysis to put them into context. Two striking and connected features of modern society are the exponential growth of science and of higher education. Both show significant steady growth from the middle of the nineteenth century and then a sudden spurt after the Second World War.

In 1985, in an influential book called *About Science*, Barry Barnes reviewed the material about the exponential growth of science since the mid-seventeenth century, noting that 'the growth of science . . . has consistently outstripped that of the resources and infrastructure needed to sustain and support it' (Barnes 1985: 4). Taking the trends in the 1960s (very significantly fuelled by military-related research), 'after another century of such growth, given our current population trends, the entire labour force would have been conscripted to science' (Barnes 1985: 4).

Both points (growth outstripping resources, and with no clear end in sight) feel very much like the experience of higher education world wide. Data collected in the West Report (Australia's version of the UK's Dearing Report of 1997), extrapolates global growth in higher education between 1990 and 2025 as likely to be 278 per cent: from 42 million students to 159 million students. Of these, the contribution from Asia is likely to rise by a massive 412 per cent: from 17 million to 87 million (cited in Dearing 1998: 1).

The motives and stimuli for the recent, very rapid expansion of higher education seem to be a mixture of political push factors (including economic competitiveness and national prestige) and social pull factors (including recognition of higher education credentials as a 'positional' good). Neither can be described as fully rational, or indeed as susceptible to traditional 'investment appraisal' analysis. The Dearing Committee struggled to find economists who could agree on the so-called 'externalities' associated with higher education. Both for governments and for individuals, investing in higher education has been something of an act of faith. Nor may their interests entirely coincide. Tom Schuller and others have pointed to the different modes of analysis and outcomes associated with the concepts of 'human capital' – strictly quantitatively analysed – and 'social capital' – much more qualitatively assessed. An approach that fixates on the individual agent, and the personal as well as collective 'rates of return' of the purchase of educational qualifications, can easily miss the impact of access to higher education on social networks and relationships, socially shaped values and norms, the strength of mutual and civic obligations, and, ultimately, the general quality of life (Schuller 1998).

Empirically however, there can be no doubt that internationally we are seeing a convergence on 'mass' systems of higher education and away from 'elite' systems, as set out most authoritatively in Martin Trow's taxonomy. For Trow, *elite* systems enrol up to 15 per cent of the age group; *mass* systems enrol 15–40 per cent of the age group; and *universal* systems enrol more than 40 per cent of the age group (Scott 1995: 2).

This well established set of benchmarks has become slightly less relevant over time. This is firstly because they ignore the 'lifelong learning' factor, in that even initial higher education is no longer the province of the uniformly prepared young (for example, most UK students in higher education are over 21 when they commence study). Secondly, they concentrate entirely on process rather than on outputs. (What happens to all of these students; to what extent do they succeed?) Taking graduation as a proxy for success in higher education, it is interesting to look at graduation rates by country. Figure 0.1 shows that on this count we have internationally several 'mass' systems, a majority in the developed world close to or over the 'mass' threshold, and very few that could any longer safely be regarded as 'elite.'

The latest Organization for Economic Cooperation and Development (OECD) figures only serve to underline this widening gap between the so-called 'efficient' and 'less efficient' systems. Taking the sample as a whole, approximately 34 per cent of each cohort enrol, but only 22 per cent graduate (a 'drop out' rate of over one third). When the UK and US samples are adjusted for this, it means that the UK now produces proportionately about the same number of graduates as the USA (Marshall 1998).

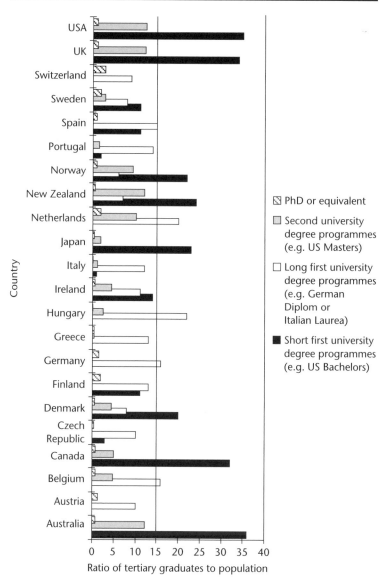

Figure 0.1   Ratio of tertiary graduates to population at the typical age of graduation (times 100) by type of programme (1996)
Source: OECD (1998)

Certain characteristics of the recent development of higher education appear to be generic if not universal. The major one, as already discussed, is the pressure for expansion, for economic as well as personal and cultural reasons. More deeply, however, it is possible to identify certain features that are almost inexorable concomitants of expansion.

Firstly, there is invariably a challenge to the 'distinctiveness' of higher education as an intellectual or epistemological enterprise. For example, the notion of a special 'idea of higher education' as argued for by Ron Barnett in an influential series of books, can be threatened by the case for a large, undifferentiated post-compulsory sector, especially with 'training' for occupational competence at its heart (Barnett 1990, 1994, 1997).

Secondly, concerns are expressed about the maintenance of standards. This is a special dilemma for both advocates and detractors of the shift from elite to mass. For example, the psychologist John Radford in a recent polemic entitled *Quantity and Quality in Higher Education*, asserts, apparently objectively, that 'to the extent that students are actually selected by ability, then more in a literal sense must mean worse'. He further notes that a 30 per cent slice of each cohort takes us down to an IQ of 115 (roughly the same level as the mean of US freshmen) (Radford *et al.* 1997: 11–12). The obvious rebuttal is that, of course, elite systems never did select on the basis of ability, either alone or, in several instances, at all in a composite of reasons for admissions decisions.

Thirdly, there is evidence of significantly greater 'instrumentality' all round, on the part of students and their sponsors, teachers, and other stakeholding 'consumers', such as employers. So-called 'educational inflation' can lead to some apparently paradoxical outcomes. For example, a group of US sociologists has recently looked at the question of *Education and Democratic Citizenship in America*. They establish that a simple additive model of educational success increases democratic tolerance but does little for social equality or improving material life-chances, and conclude with a riveting question: 'Does competition for educational advantage result in more education than we can afford?' As in a competitive framework for social position, educational attainment rates are pressed higher and higher, 'in this way, individual rationality may be leading to collective irrationality' (Nie *et al.* 1996: 194–6).

Fourthly, there is hot debate about institutional status; both 'stratification' and the acceptable 'limits of diversity'. On the principle of the greener grass on the other side of the fence, discussion of this issue often reduces to simple advocacy of other national models, with greater emphasis on their advantages rather than their disadvantages.

It is important to recognize that these different national models come as packages. If you want the US 'market'-driven, system you get not only an immense diversity of institutions (by price, quality and mission), but also a pattern of professional formation much more dependent on postgraduate education, and, critically, regularly deferred completion of qualifications. Similarly, if you want the mainstream 'European' model of very large municipal institutions with relatively low thresholds for entry and high social 'entitlements' for students, you also get highly restricted student access to facilities (such as libraries), poor rates of progression and relatively low completion of degrees (Watson 1998: 74–6).

Finally, there is controversy about how the increasing costs of ever larger systems should be met, focused especially on the identification and 'charging' of the beneficiaries. This issue is often cast in terms of the 'marketization' or 'privatization' of higher education (Williams 1997), but it is very important to remember that higher education rarely attains the status of a pure or true market (the US model is perhaps the closest, with Japan a little behind). To take just three counter instances: only in the most perverse instances can 'student-consumers' simply purchase awards; there are no whole systems that are entirely independent of public investment, and hence of external accountability; while, such is the social position of the providing institutions, that market failure is only very reluctantly tolerated.

Each national system will have developed its own angle or 'spin' on each of these. The test that follows – of specifically UK based examples of the dilemmas of higher education growth – could be easily replicated in a variety of national settings.

On *distinctiveness* the UK has made the firm policy decision (principally through the 1992 Further and Higher Education Act) to move professional and vocational higher education into the mainstream. It has also elected to build up and expand its historical strengths in continuing education and continuing professional development. Peter Scott has characterized the result as the 'abandonment of class distinctions between different types of higher education':

> In much of the rest of Europe, universities have clung to a highly 'academic' mission in which practicality has been ignored, while 'inferior' institutions have been boxed into an inflexible vocationalism. In Britain, the whole idea of a university has been refreshed, the horizons of the traditional universities have been enlarged and the aspirations of the former polytechnics have been raised.
>
> (Scott 1999: 2)

Another outcome has been calls for the blurring of the boundaries between all types of post-compulsory education, and between further and higher education in particular. Interestingly, the Dearing Committee of 1996–97 (discussed in Chapter 1) resisted this, and clung to a vision of the essence of higher education, especially in self-reflective and self-critical practice. The kind of dialogue between staff and students, as more or less experienced participants in a process of learning, are thus felt to be as applicable to professional and vocational pursuits at the higher levels as to traditional academic subjects (National Committee of Inquiry into Higher Education (NCIHE) 1997: Chapter 8).

In contrast, the government appears to be at least ambivalent on this question. It is instructive to search the recent response documents and the Lifelong Learning Green Paper for the places where 'further and higher education' are used together, and when separately (Department for Education and Employment (DfEE) 1998a, 1998b, 1998c). The former include almost every reference to funding, and hence imply that in the Treasury's thinking in particular a merged system is in favour.

This links with the questions about *standards*. Here the UK story gives an interesting counterpoint to some of the gloom-merchants. Expansion has clearly not used up the pool of people with what Robbins called, in a famous phrase, 'the ability to benefit' from higher education. The evidence from degree outcomes and from peer assessment is incontrovertible. It is, however, countered by a largely anecdotal and emotional series of charges that, in another evocative phrase, 'more means worse' or 'dumbing down'. Such charges often confuse issues about the quality of life within increasingly financially pressed institutions, and about the changing map of knowledge in the modern world, with those of the real performance of the system in a changing environment (Watson and Taylor 1998: 74–9).

Changed content does indeed link with increased *instrumentality*, and student-led demand does indeed reflect a swing to greater vocational and career sensitivity on the part of students. This is, of course, rational behaviour. As discussed above, in the more elite, restricted system of the past, graduates achieved market salience simply by having a degree, especially from a prestigious institution. In a world where a third of new workforce entrants are graduates, the nature of the degree and its immediate purchase on the requirements of employers is obviously more central. Equally, the logic of social investment implies the development *within work* of more effective use of better qualified people. This is at least one answer, painful though the period of adjustment may be, to questions about graduate under-employment. This confidence in (perhaps it would be safer to call it a gamble on) the capacity of education to help 'grow the job' is not a new idea. I have so far been able to trace it back at least as far as Alfred Marshall's *Principles of Economics* of 1890 (Marshall 1890: 175–6).

Larger systems also raise questions of *institutional status*. Purely market-driven systems quickly produce and then embed rankings and a rigid pecking order; other systems rely much more on the state to fix and maintain strata of institutions (usually by policing the academic/professional divide). The UK experiment is about collective responsibility for the limits of a plural system of institutions, very much in line with its own historical development, although this has left us with an apparently very muddled pattern of institutions (Scott 1995: 44–9).

Finally there are the questions of *funding*. Internationally we are now dealing with the aftermath of governments' attempts to secure what they invariably regard as a more even-handed basis for contributions by the beneficiaries of higher education (that is, students and their sponsors). One interesting exercise is to monitor the extent, nature and effect of protest against this shift in various societies. So far, at least, the UK is well towards the passive end of the scale (Neave 1998).

In addition to such 'universal' or 'generic' pressures any national system will possess 'exceptional' features of its own history and context that influence the outcome in its own case. In the UK three such features dominate.

Firstly, there is the huge and continuing influence of class and economic stratification. The most recent surge of expansion in higher education, which gave us what Richard Taylor and I have termed the 'post-Baker system', has made huge differences in the internal population of universities in terms of gender, age, ethnicity and even disability, but only the tiniest inroads on working-class participation (Watson and Taylor 1998: 3–9, 27–9).

Secondly, the UK experiences both the benefits and disadvantages of what is called, in the sphere of economic history, 'first phase industrialism' – of having contributed to creating the model of the university that is internationally recognized but has come to be subtly and imaginatively customized in other national contexts, including in ways apparently not available to the pioneers (this pathology is, of course, not unique to Great Britain – it may be to Europe).

Thirdly, we are prisoners of a political and social culture that is both institutionally conservative and suspicious of experimentation, especially with public money. Scott comments further on how little 'celebration' there has been of UK achievements through higher education reform. 'Britain seems to have acquired a mass system of higher education in a fit of guilty absent-mindedness' (Scott 1999: 2). This may connect with the system's apparently high capacity for internal adjustment without major protest.

Both the 'global' and the 'national' developments set out above present constraints and opportunities for the development of individual university and college strategies.

1

EXTERNAL PERSPECTIVES

Stakeholders

One of the key problems in setting a strategic framework for a college or university is that the individual institution has both positive and negative constraints placed upon its freedom of action. Most importantly in the UK it sits within a 'sector' of higher education that claims to act cohesively and collectively on major issues (such as the confirmation of academic standards). This sector has its own identity through representative bodies such as the Committee of Vice-Chancellors and Principals (CVCP) and the Standing Committee of Principals (SCOP). External stakeholders like the Funding Councils (FCs) will also wish to relate to the sector and its strategy as well as to individual higher education institutions (HEIs).

Other groups also take a sector-wide view. For example 'higher education' as a whole relates to other phases of the education service (schools and further education) as well as to a set of other public services (health, social services and so on) with interests in it as a source of both research and the professional formation of their personnel. Standing behind these interests are government departments other than the DfEE. These include not only the Department of Health and the Department of Social Security, but also the Department of Trade and Industry, the Department of the Environment, Transport and the Regions, the Ministry of Defence, the Home Office and the Office of Science and Technology. Less formally, organizations of employers (like the Confederation of British Industry (CBI), Institute of Directors (IOD) and the Association of Graduate Recruiters (AGR)) and of employees (trade unions and professional bodies such as the new Institute for Learning and Teaching (ILT)) feel that they have authoritative standing in matters of higher education direction and delivery. Meanwhile, 'hybrid' groups, such as the Council for Industry and Higher Education (CIHE) seek to broker positive relationships between such varied stakeholders.

The bottom line is that, in the absence of a single, specific set of 'shareholders', there is a panoply of 'stakeholders', each of whom can, with varying degrees of legitimacy (all of which can, however, be traced back to tax-paying), claim to 'own' a piece of higher education and its outcomes. When this is mapped on to the macrocosm of the higher education system and the microcosm of the notionally independent college or university, the potential for mixed messages, for disappointment and for only partially informed external criticism is legion.

To give an example of the DfEE's own perception of stakeholding, Table 1.1 lists the bodies consulted in 1998 about its 'prior options' review of the Higher Education Funding Council for England (HEFCE) (DfEE 1998d).

A charitable view of this list is that it underlines the difficulties of stakeholder analysis, in terms of both categorization and comprehensiveness. A more sinister conclusion is that it shows how easily the process can become ideologically loaded. Why, for example, include these pressure groups and not others (the Council for Academic Autonomy but not Save British Science)? Why include these subject groups and professional and statutory bodies (heavily directed towards health) and not others (no Engineering Council or Central Committee for the Education of Social Workers)? Why ignore the government departments that are heavy purchasers of research (Ministry of Defence, Home Office, Ministry of Agriculture, Fisheries and Food)? Why ignore some recognized trade unions (Manufacturing, Science and Finance (MSF))? Taken as a whole, however, the list says some interesting things about the shape of the sector as seen from the DfEE's elegant headquarters in Sanctuary Buildings, Westminster.

Scanning the horizon

A primary function of strategic management is thus monitoring the developing positions of all of these other 'influentials' and sorting out how both the sector and the institution may be placed to cope with them.

Governments tend to alternate waves of activism with lulls of inertia in terms of higher education policy. This was certainly the case in the UK with the 1979–97 Conservative government's creation of an apparently mass system of higher education for the UK (Watson

Table 1.1 DfEE/HEFCE 'stakeholders'

Higher education or further education institutional representative bodies	Other government departments	Other organizations	Trade unions	Student organizations	Employer representative bodies	Professional bodies
Committee of Vice-Chancellors and Principals	Department of Health/NHS Executive	Universities and Colleges Admissions Service	Public and Commercial Services Union	National Union of Students	Confederation of British Industry	British Medical Association
Standing Committee of Principals	Department of Trade and Industry	Further Education Funding Council	Association of University Teachers	SKILL: National Bureau for Students with Disabilities	Engineering Employers' Federation	British Dental Association
Committee of University Chairmen	Office of Science and Technology	Higher Education Funding Council for Wales	National Association of Teachers and Further and Higher Education	The Open University Students' Association	Institute of Directors	Royal College of Nursing
Association of Colleges	National Audit Office	Scottish Higher Education Funding Council	UNISON			Council for Professions Supplementary to Medicine
Universities and Colleges Employers Association	Department of the Environment, Transport and the Regions (for Government Offices)	The Higher Education Statistics Agency	Trades Union Congress			Royal Institution of British Architects

Table 1.1 (cont d)

Higher education or further education institutional representative bodies	Other government departments	Other organizations	Trade unions	Student organizations	Employer representative bodies	Professional bodies
Association of Heads of University Administrators	Department of Education, Northern Ireland	Teacher Training Agency	Transport and General Workers Union			Chartered Institute of Public Finance and Accounting
British Universities Finance Directors Group	Department for Culture, Media and Sport	The British Academy				Joint Committee of the Bar Council and the Law Society
Council of University Deans of Arts and Humanities		The British Council				
Council of Churches [sic] and Associated Colleges		Museum and Galleries Commission				
Association of University Directors of Estates		Standing Conference of National and University Libraries				
University [sic] Association for Continuing Education		Society for Research into Higher Education				
Council of Heads of Medical Schools		Training and Enterprise National Council				
Council for Academic Autonomy		Local Government Association				
		Council for Industry and Higher Education				

and Bowden 1999). The current Labour government's enthusiasm for lifelong learning, and the flurry of decision and consultation from February of 1998 provides another rich mixture of opportunities and threats for higher education. An analysis of this rapidly changing policy environment provides a useful test case of a national system's exposure to the political world.

In September 1993, Secretary of State for Education John Patten aroused outrage by suggesting to vice-chancellors that it was not his place to think strategically about higher education. His more emollient successor, Gillian Shephard, was more open to advice and commissioned a departmental review of higher education in 1994, which never reported. Instead it was swept away in an avalanche of re-evaluation and advice, notably following the bipartisan establishment of the NCIHE (the Dearing Committee) in 1996 (Watson and Bowden 1999). The immediate cause was a threatened revolt by vice-chancellors, who planned to address a crisis of underfunded expansion by charging 'top-up' or 'registration' fees. The political imperative was to keep the emotive issue of the apparent end of 'free' full-time higher education out of the upcoming election campaign.

The Dearing Report's terms of reference were dauntingly wide:

> To make recommendations on how the purposes, shape, structure, size and funding of higher education, including support for students, should develop to meet the needs of the United Kingdom over the next 20 years, recognising that higher education embraces teaching, learning, scholarship and research.
>
> (NCIHE 1997: 3)

A set of supplementary 'principles' included the ominous instruction to have 'regard' to 'the Government's other spending priorities and affordability' (NCIHE 1997: 3). This was all to be done 'by the summer of 1997'.

In due course, and as the result of parallel initiatives by the Further Education Funding Council (FEFC) on widening participation (through a committee chaired by Helena Kennedy) and the DfEE, which established a working group on lifelong learning chaired by Bob Fryer, the Labour government, elected in May 1997, received early advice from:

- the Kennedy Report, *Learning Works: Widening Participation in Further Education*, in June (Kennedy 1997);
- the Dearing Report, *Higher Education in the Learning Society*, in July (NCIHE 1997); and

- the Report of the Fryer Committee, *Learning for the Twenty-first Century*, in November (Fryer 1997).

They published their response in February 1998 in three papers:

- a Green Paper, *The Learning Age: A Renaissance for a New Britain* (DfEE 1998a);
- a response to the Dearing Report, *Higher Education for the 21st Century* (DfEE 1998b); and
- a response to the Kennedy Report, *Further Education for the New Millennium* (DfEE 1998c).

In *Learning Works* (Kennedy 1997) the key ideas were:

- equity in access, particularly for those who have so far played no role in the post-compulsory system;
- the need to focus on achievement at Level 3 ('A' level equivalent) in particular;
- re-prioritization of funding, plus potential use of the National Lottery; and
- overcoming inefficiency and waste in administration and funding, as well as the benefits system.

The main arguments in *Higher Education in the Learning Society* (NCIHE 1997) were for:

- the contribution of higher education to an integrated system of lifelong learning;
- a new vision for learning and teaching in higher education;
- funding research properly, and according to its intended outcomes; and
- the new compact between students and their sponsors, institutions and government (representing the national interest) (Watson and Taylor 1998: 151–2).

The core argument in *Learning for the Twenty-first Century* (Fryer 1997) was for the establishment of a universal 'learning culture'. Beyond this, it is a little cruel, but I think fair, to say that its big idea was to have no big ideas; it is just a compendium of little ones. Given that it was set up to presage a White Paper on lifelong learning, it performed a valuable role in compiling lists of initiatives that have worked or could work, with no real prioritization or costings.

The three papers related to the DfEE ministerial team then in place in some interesting ways. The Secretary of State, David Blunkett, resonated most strongly with the Kennedy Report and its passionate analysis of deficit. The Parliamentary Under-Secretary, Kim Howells, who then formally held the lifelong learning brief, had to make sense of the array of ideas in Fryer, and to choose from them, as he did in *The Learning Age* (DfEE 1998a). Meanwhile, deeply conscious of her role as a former head of an HEI (Birkbeck College, London), Minister of State Tessa Blackstone steered Dearing into a kind of no man's land, between the Treasury and the CVCP.

The Green Paper (DfEE 1998a) concentrated on six key initiatives, with a host of proposals for related activity (references are to paragraph numbers). The key initiatives were: Individual Learning Accounts [2.10ff.] (with a £150 million pilot project); the University for Industry [1.6ff.] (to be launched in late 1999), along with its associated helpline, 'Learning Direct' [1.16ff.]; the educational implications of the New Deal (including extension to those aged over 25) [3.28]; a strong focus on basic skills (especially through the Basic Skills Agency) [3.25]; the National Grid for Learning [1.26]; and plans for an additional 500,000 students in further and higher education.

Among the associated initiatives and changes to new and existing agencies were: the British Educational Communications and Technology Agency (BECTA) [1.23]; 'BBC Learning' [1.24]; Graduate Apprenticeships [2.15, 3.13], 'National Traineeships' [2.27] and additional Modern Apprenticeships [3.29]; a raft of student support possibilities, including extension of loans to over-50s [2.22], abolition of the disabled means test [2.24], extension of career development loans [2.26], and childcare [2.30]; legislation on 16–17-year-olds in work (to be supported to National Vocational Qualification (NVQ) level 2) [3.3]; retention of the two remaining industrial training boards [3.4]; further consultation on National Education and Training Targets (NETTs) [3.6]; a National Skills Task Force [3.22]; the prospect of further national training organizations [3.34]; Investing in Young People (IiYP) [4.4]; additional resources for the statutory careers service [4.8]; the youth service to be put on a statutory basis [4.9]; a Committee on Education for Citizenship and the Teaching of Democracy [4.10]; an Adult and Community Learning Fund [4.19]; a New Deal for disabled people [4.36]; funds for digital content in public libraries [4.38]; an advisory group on creativity and innovation [4.40]; a collaborative fund for post-16 education [4.44]; using the European Union (EU) Presidency of mid 1997 and the European Social Fund [4.48–9]; a new Training Standards Council (to police Training and Enterprise Councils (TECs)) [5.9]; Records of Achievement (ROAs) [6.7]; and the establishment of a national Credit Accumulation and Transfer Scheme (CATS) by 2000 [6.18].

One reaction to this list is how undiscriminating it was about the locus of responsibility, and how silent on coordination. A more positive message was that we all have a part to play: government departments, Regional Development Agencies (RDAs) [6.7], Local Education Authorities (LEAs), institutions, employers, voluntary agencies and individuals.

In section 4.28 the paper set out a vision for higher education institutions, as follows:

> We wish universities, higher and further education to be beacons of learning in their local communities. At today's participation rates, 60 per cent of school-leavers can expect to enter higher education at some time in their lives. We propose that higher education should play an even bigger part in future by:
>
> - providing more places to meet demand;
> - offering a wide range of courses up to postgraduate level;
> - ensuring high standards so as to enhance the employability of graduates;
> - improving participation by offering opportunities later in life to those who missed out first time around;
> - contributing more to the economy and being more responsive to the needs of business;
> - collaborating effectively with other institutions, other learning providers and with the world of work; and
> - making itself more accessible by exploiting new technology and flexible delivery with facilities available at times convenient to students.
>
> (DfEE 1998a: 4.28)

Other specific further education [5.4ff.] and higher education [5.14ff.] points were picked up in the responses to the Kennedy Report and the Dearing Report.

Higher Education for the 21st Century (DfEE 1998b) throughout acknowledged and endorsed key ideas in the Dearing Report, including the funding gap, support for diversity and the 'compact'. At key points, however, it was critically non-committal pending the Comprehensive Spending Review (CSR) of the summer of 1998.

On supporting institutions the paper: confirmed the intention to restrict the efficiency gain for 1998–99 to 1 per cent [intro.]; left the question of Dearing's proposed 'reviews' by the governing body with the 'h.e. sector' [9.5], but with the FCs 'monitoring' to see if a 'condition of funding' threat became necessary [9.7]; encouraged an 'independent element' in complaints [9.8]; and held out some hope for improved general funding – 'public spending on education should increase as a proportion of national income, as the cost of social and economic failure is addressed' [10.1]. Dearing's suggestion of a three-year planning horizon for funding was left to the CSR [10.3].

On supporting students the paper: endorsed 'widening provision' – seen as a priority for extra places in 1998–99 [1.3], as well as encouraging relevant HEFC 'projects' [1.5]; confirmed the doubling, and the liberalization of 'access funds' [1.6]; announced the partial ending of means testing on the Disabled Students Allowance [1.7]; justified the approach taken (as announced in the previous July) on grants, loans and fees [10.7]; announced further research on the information needs of applicants as well as those already in higher education [2.5]; outlawed 'top-up' fees [10.9]; promised to 'monitor' students' financial situation [10.13]; promised to review the Job-seekers' Allowance (JSA) [10.15]; and delayed a decision on the Single Student Support Agency until 2000 [10.20]. Many of these elements (especially on fees and loans) were eventually given statutory power by the 1998 Teaching and Higher Education Act. The CSR was handed the tricky issue of student loans counting against the Public Sector Borrowing Requirement.

On teaching and curriculum development the paper: endorsed the establishment of the ILT, including for the accreditation of higher education teachers [3.1, 8.1, 8.2] and the kitemarking of courseware [7.10]; proposed a national scheme for electronic distribution of outstanding teaching [3.4, 7.11]; supported the development of 'core skills', including through projects on 'employability' [3.6, 6.6] and 'entrepreneurship' [6.5], as well as in research training [5.12]; encouraged development of the Progress File [3.7]; specifically left quality and standards with 'higher education as a whole', especially through the QAA [Ch. 4] (interestingly *The Learning Age* (DfEE 1998a) proposed a funding reward for high achievement in teaching [5.16]); and repeated the desire for a qualifications framework and a national credit system by 2000 [4.2].

Meanwhile additional investment in information and commun-ications technologies (ICT) [7.3], including universal access to the 'networked desktop computer' [7.8], was left to the CSR.

On the pattern of institutions the paper: envisaged sub-degree growth 'mainly but not exclusively' in further education, but also 'no significant growth in degrees' in further education [1.8]; was less firm than the Dearing Report on the problems of multiple and serial franchising [4.9]; hid behind the Committee of University Chairmen (CUC) on tricky questions like composition of governing bodies [9.1] and terms of office [9.3], but offered quick response on proposed changes to articles of governance [9.4]; threatened institutions using names to which they are not entitled [9.9]; endorsed the Dearing Report definition of a 'university college' (fully a part of a university or with taught-degree powers) [9.10]; proposed 'relative stability' in the number of universities [9.11] and declared an intention to consult on criteria for new ones [9.12]; and opened up the possibility of a Funding Council in Northern Ireland [11.8].

On supporting communities the paper: promised higher education representation on RDAs and FEFC regional committees [6.1]; and announced the continuation of the Higher Education Regional Development Fund (HERDF) in England [6.2]. Issues like funds for incubator units and equity stake in spin-outs [6.4] were left to the CSR.

On research the paper: wished to see the research assessment exercise (RAE) extending beyond peer review (to other 'users') [5.3]; was silent on the Dearing Report's proposals about scholarship funding and the opt-out (hiding behind the FCs own consultation); and rejected an independent advisory body (offering a possible revival of the Council for Science and Technology) [5.11].

The CSR was left to deal with the case made for dual funding top-up [5.1], the Industrial Development Partnership Fund [5.6], and the Arts and Humanities Research Council [5.10].

Other points of interest included: support for a post-qualifications admissions process (PQA) in principle [2.1]; a very strong puff for Investors in People (IIP) [8.3]; a strong resolve to leave pay and conditions as 'a matter for employers' [8.5]; some thoughts about how the review of the teachers' pension scheme could include a transfer of all university staff to Universities Superannuation Scheme (USS) [8.6]; reluctance to follow the Dearing Report's strong line on the possible withdrawal of degree-awarding powers [9.13]; deferral of the vexed issue of (primarily) Oxford and Cambridge 'college fees' [10.4]; a resolution to 'keep in mind' future independent advisory committees [10.26]; and a fudge on the fee liability for Scottish fourth year [11.2], which in 1998 briefly threatened the passage of the Teaching and Higher Education Act.

In *Further Education for the New Millennium* (DfEE 1998c), the Kennedy Report received much praise for its vision, but little else. Instead, issues were swept into the Green Paper (DfEE 1998a) and the CSR, while the Level 3 priority was largely dismissed.

Key points included: the assertion that addressing Level 3 will be addressed by getting Level 2 right [2.4, 5.4]; the focus on partnerships and collaboration to be achieved through RDAs and the Further Education Collaboration Fund [3.1]; an announcement that the CSR would include 'options for creating greater equity in post-16 funding' [4.2, 4.7]; a statement that it was 'too early' to make firm decisions on the post-Millennium Lottery Fund [4.5]; the suggestion that employer contributions would be pulled through Individual Learning Accounts (ILAs) [4.8]; an advisory group to be established to monitor LEA discretionary grants [5.2]; amendment of JSA rules so that 'those over 25 who have been unemployed for more than two years can study full-time for up to a year without having to be available for employment in term-time' [5.6]; harmonization of post-16 inspectorate [6.2]; rejection of a new 'learners' charter', at least until the JSA review is completed [7.2]; and reluctance to take on any of the ideas about tax reform [2.5, 3.2].

As suggested above, together these documents (DfEE 1998a,b,c) provide a probably uniquely full test case for strategic reading of advice to a government and of its response. The sector and individual institutions would ignore these messages at their peril. Combining them with the specific outcomes of the CSR, the position almost two years after the Dearing Report seems to be a firm 'two cheers' from the institutions for the government. New funding has been found (although not confirmed for three years at the time of writing) to enable the 1 per cent annual efficiency target to be met. Substantial funding (up to £1.1 billion including matching funding from the Wellcome Foundation) has been promised for research over the planning period. Simultaneously commitments to a return to expansion and to widened participation have been made, although the vexed question of the boundary between further and higher education remains unresolved. An Arts and Humanities Research Board has been created (through an amalgamation of Funding Council and British Academy resources). But the fundamental problem of teaching infrastructure (especially building and investment in ICT) has yet to be tackled frontally (DfEE 1998e).

Similar forensic attention is valuable when applied to purchasers and funders, especially the FCs. The FCs are also, of course, simultaneously trying to read the minds of political masters, and are given at least annual 'directions' from the relevant Secretaries of State. For example, the DfEE letter of 'guidance' to the HEFCE on 'higher education funding for 1999–00 and beyond' includes detailed elaboration of the following 12 'Secretary of State's priorities': evaluation; quality and standards; increasing participation; widening access; employability; collaboration; capital and information technology (IT) infrastructure; Private Finance Initiative (PFI)/public–private partnerships (PPPs); research; financial management; sustainable development; and Year 2000 (DfEE 1998f: 2–8).

In this process the FCs, like the institutions, are rarely given instructions that are crystal clear, and can be dealt policy hands that are frankly contradictory. In this way politicians can often pass on responsibility for resolving paradoxes or evade direct responsibility for unintended consequences. A classic example of such 'delegated' responsibility was the drive throughout the late 1980s and early 1990s for both increased efficiency (largely achieved by unfunded expansion) and preservation of traditional measures of quality. As specifically 'arms-length' bodies, the FCs will sort out these messages through a combination of conditions and incentives attached to core funding and special programmes and initiatives (almost always involving competitive bidding).

Thus the HEFCE's 'corporate plan' for 1998–2001 sets out a 'mission' statement: 'to promote high quality, cost effective teaching and research within a financially healthy higher education sector, having regard to national needs' (HEFCE 1998a). A successor document (the 'strategic plan' for 1999–2004) then identifies 11 key strategic aims (with a healthy abundance of what Peter Womack calls 'superegoic verbs', 1999: 3):

- develop and sustain effective partnerships with institutions, employers, other funding and professional bodies, and others with a stake in higher education, by providing clear and open information and promoting collaboration between them;
- advise Government and other stakeholders on higher education's needs and aspirations, and help make widely known the achievements and opportunities offered by higher education, particularly to students;
- promote and support productive interaction between HE and industry and commerce in order to encourage the transfer of knowledge and expertise and enhance the relevance of programmes of teaching and research to the needs of employers and the economy;
- promote high standards of education so as to advance knowledge and scholarship, encourage improvement, enterprise and innovation, and enhance students' learning experiences and employment prospects;
- promote high standards of research so as to advance knowledge and scholarship and encourage improvement, enterprise and innovation;
- use consultation, research and benchmarking to increase knowledge and understanding of higher education, and inform policy development;
- promote effective financial management, accountability for the use of public funds, and value for money;
- contribute to the healthy development of higher education in the country and overseas by learning from international

experience, and helping to promote the reputation of UK higher education abroad;
- encourage institutions to increase access, secure equal opportunities, support lifelong learning, and maximise achievement for all who can benefit from higher education;
- maintain and encourage the development of a wide variety of institutions, with a diversity of missions that build upon their local, regional, national and international strengths, and are responsive to change within a financially healthy sector;
- enable our staff to provide a high quality service, within an open and supportive working environment.

(HEFCE 1999a: 3)

The FCs simultaneously perform an important role in analysing institutional strategic plans in gross. In doing so they can often reveal the long-standing tension in educational policy between the 'individual' rationality of uncoordinated institutional action and the subsequent 'collective' irrationality of the combined effect (Thurow 1972). In analysing the last set of plans before Dearing reported they discovered, for example:

- 60 per cent of institutions promised more flexibility in course delivery (through part-time and mixed mode study, open and distance learning, work-based programmes and so on);
- 60 per cent of institutions had formal access policies;
- 90 per cent of institutions had strategies for research (including 65 per cent referring to inter- and multi-disciplinary approaches, and 50 per cent to external collaboration – interestingly, only 20 per cent mentioned internal inter-departmental collaboration);
- 90 per cent described their 'local or regional role'; and
- 80 per cent described their 'international links'.

All of the above responses could be said to have been specifically prompted by HEFCE questions. Perhaps more interesting is the data on aggregate plans for staff and student numbers. The sector as a whole planned to recruit above its maximum aggregate student numbers (MASNs) (the number of official 'award-holders' the government was prepared to fund) by 0.7 per cent in 1998–99 (well within the official margin of 2 per cent). But thereafter collectively it saw annual growth of 1 per cent in full-time undergraduate students, 2 per cent in part-time students, 17 per cent by 2000–01 in postgraduate taught numbers, and a staggering 24 per cent in overseas full fee-paying students by the same year. The tendency for all institutions to think that they can win in all of the markets all of the time goes on apace. Meanwhile, over the same period, they saw staff numbers contracting by 1.8 per cent (1.15 per cent for 'academic' staff and 2.3 per cent for others) (HEFCE 1998b).

The outcome is a 'twin-track' need for both the sector (especially through representative bodies like the CVCP, which has dramatically improved its capacity in this regard) and for individual institutions to 'scan the horizon'. Major developmental issues (for example, the challenge of global competitiveness, or the pace of change in ICT) will have an impact at both levels. For example, the CVCP *Corporate Plan 1999–02* sets out 'to be the leading voice of UK universities' by:

- promoting public understanding of the objectives, achievements, needs and diversity of UK universities
- improving the funding, regulatory and marketing environment within which UK universities pursue their diverse missions
- assisting in the development of good practice in all spheres of university activity by sharing ideas and experience
- championing the independence and autonomy of UK universities.

(CVCP 1998a: 5)

Not all messages are top-down. The sector acts to send its own messages back, as for example in the CVCP's annual advice to the DfEE and the Treasury on the annual spending round. The fact that this advice is public means that it is at least as much about winning friends within the wider political community, and reassuring colleagues within the institutions, as about expecting the paymaster seriously to think again (CVCP 1998b).

Operating in this quasi-political environment, it is also important to ensure that messages sent do not rebound: either by being wilfully misunderstood or by having a bluff called. Two examples of the latter are when the English institutions thought that they would break the HEFCE system of teaching quality assessment (TQA) by demanding 'universal' visiting, and when the CVCP thought that independent analysis of Research Council overheads would support their case for an increase. In the former case, the Funding Council further frustrated the institutions by giving them what they wanted (Watson 1995). In the latter case a report by Coopers and Lybrand was quickly shelved when it emerged that many institutions had no real idea of what their overheads were (Coopers and Lybrand 1998).

Patterns of bilateral and sub-sectoral alliance are also important here. Journalists enjoy identifying, and trying to drive wedges between, the different 'groupings' of universities; especially the research-rich

Russell group and the essentially reactive 'Coalition of Modern Universities', which was started by a set of post-1992 universities to emphasize both the 'teaching' and 'widening participation' priorities to which denizens of the Russell Hotel (from which the name derives) were apparently less committed. The Coalition of Modern Universities has recently hired professional lobbyists, to uncertain effect (Major 1998). But there are other groups as well: those with medical schools; the '94' group of post-Robbins universities; the South Coast 'Channel Islands Consortium', and so on. Higher education lobbying is a fraught and complex field despite the apparent advantage it should enjoy, with such a high proportion of graduates (of a restricted range of institutions) in influential public positions.

Putting the messages of the Dearing Report, the government, the FCs and the representative bodies together, a set of priorities emerge that individual institutions in the UK (whatever their separate mission priorities) seem unlikely to be able to ignore. This 'inescapable agenda' includes:

- access and widening participation (it is apparently no longer acceptable for elite institutions and competitive courses to be so overwhelmingly dominated by the affluent privately prepared);
- funding (where the system is now converging on a broad assumption of equal funding for equal work);
- community links (why should the walls around the ivory tower be higher and its treasures more exclusively guarded?);
- collaboration and partnerships (including across the further/higher education boundary – as will be required by sector-wide acknowledgement of credit);
- the scholarly environment (which the Dearing Report argued is essential for genuinely higher education and which the government has apparently preserved by rejecting the notion of the 'teaching-only' university first mooted in the mid-1980s (Advisory Board for the Research Councils (ABRC) 1987)); and
- attention to quality and standards (where the whole theory of the about-to-be-reinvigorated external examiner system is that closed-shops, rings and isolation of groups should not be allowed to emerge). (See Watson 1999: 333.)

The contributors to Lockwood and Davies's *Universities: the Management Challenge* (1985: 1–23) listed seven 'challenges' for managers in future. Looking back over a decade and a half it is salutary to reflect on their 'hits' and 'misses'.

'The first challenge is the most obvious, the fact of contraction.' A clear 'miss', not even accurate for higher education as a whole at the

time of writing, as the public sector of higher education had already embarked upon the expansion that would, by the time of the ending of the binary line seven years later, make it the majority contributor.

'The second challenge is the major constraint of the comparative loss of autonomy of the universities.' For the 'university' sector of the time an undeniable hit, as the University Grants Committee (UGC) was swallowed into first the Universities Funding Council (UFC) and then the 'merged' territorial FCs from 1988 onwards; again for the polytechnics and colleges, freed from local authority control by incorporation under the same Education Reform Act, the reverse was almost precisely true.

'Third is the growth of uncertainty.' A palpable hit, across the whole of higher education.

'The fourth challenge is to become more efficient.' Almost an understatement given the dramatic drop in the level of public funding per student driven into the system by the Conservative government of 1979–97 – initially in the public sector only, but from the late 1980s across the board; nor does the process have any prospect of finishing as even the Dearing Report juxtaposed its analysis of a funding crisis in the late 1990s with a recognition that, given infrastructural restoration, the sector should enter the next millennium anticipating annual efficiency gains of around 1 per cent.

'The fifth challenge is that of the market.' Another mixed outcome, as certainly 'consumer' pressure on the system has grown; this is, however, offset by current strenuous efforts to restore confidence in the consistent standard of the 'product' and the universal currency of awards.

'In this environment, the sixth challenge for the universities is the creation and maintenance of flexibility.' Probably the most consistently successful prediction, as seen in the 'worked example' of strategic planning in the Appendix.

'The seventh major challenge is for the universities to manage all changes required of them without excessive damage to the morale of their staffs.' Another hit, possibly only to be modified by the development of a wider definition of 'staff' involved in directly supporting the enterprise than was regularly envisaged by traditional universities a decade and a half ago.

(Lockwood and Davies 1985: 19–20)

So, overall, this was an impressive scanning exercise. It needs to be modified in 1999 by substituting for number one the reciprocal challenge of continued expansion, by updating number two to deal with post-binary realities, and by adding the eighth, ninth and tenth challenges of regionalization, globalization and maintenance of sector-wide reputation for quality and standards. Lockwood and Davies might now continue as follows:

> '*The eighth challenge is to understand and respond to local and not just national and international demands.*' All HEIs, including those that have historically proved most aloof, now have to engage directly with local and emerging regional government, not least through the new English RDAs, and meet the challenges summarized by the CVCP in their report *Universities and Communities* (CVCP 1994).
>
> '*The ninth challenge is to recognize and adapt to the implications of higher education as a global enterprise.*' Higher education has not only become a global business, estimated to be worth over £9b to the UK balance of trade, but UK HEIs have also to maintain this strong performance alongside a historical commitment to the use of higher education – and the global medium of the English language – as a means of international cooperation and development (Bennell 1998; Scott 1998: 108–30).
>
> '*The tenth challenge is to understand those aspects of the national and international reputation of the UK higher education sector where institutions must act firmly, collectively and transparently, especially with regard to quality and standards.*' As indicated in the international survey in the Introduction, the UK has made the bold decision to attempt to maintain a unified higher education system, with academic responsibility for 'enlargement' as well as the maintenance of standards entrusted to peer review (Watson and Taylor 1998: 74–9).

Competition, collaboration and complementarity

The speed with which the external environment can change is well represented by the change in official rhetoric between the Conservative government of 1979–97 and its Labour successor. Before May 1997 officially sponsored competition was seen as the way to inspire innovation and efficiency. Now the same goals are seen as inhering in inter-institutional collaboration. The final step, of ensuring planned complementarity of mission between institutions (especially on a regional basis) has yet to come.

The history of collaborative ventures in UK higher education has not been impressive. Certainly the largest and most expensive such initiative to date – the Management and Administrative Computing (MAC) initiative, which ran from 1988 until 1995 at a cost of over

£7 million – ended in tears, with, in the independent reviewer's words, a failure to 'deliver what was expected'. The review team went on to identify five 'important lessons about collaboration' as follows:

- Collaborative groupings must generally be voluntary, with no element of moral compulsion to participate.
- Collaboration tends to work best on a small scale.
- Collaborative groupings work better if they have shared interests and philosophies, and geographical proximity is useful.
- Whatever the size of the collaborative grouping it must have clear project management processes and disciplines, by which members must agree to be bound.
- Members must accept that they will not be able to obtain all of their user requirements from a collaborative project and will have to undertake in-house adaptation on their own for a considerable proportion of what they need.

(Mason 1998: 13, 16)

Perhaps the key lesson about collaboration and 'partnership' (another mantra of the turn of the century), is that both proceed best when they are not entered into either to overcome perceived weakness or to maximize felt advantage. The mutually desired 'third thing' or shared objective is at the heart of successful shared enterprises.

In the spirit of this conclusion the universities of Brighton and Sussex have certainly been trying. For the past decade a Joint Planning Group consisting of the most senior managers of the two institutions (directorate from Brighton, vice- and pro-vice chancellors and registrar from Sussex) has met termly to review strategy, to identify opportunities, and to seek to ensure that inter-institutional competition does not become destructive. There have been hits: notably collaboration over links with the NHS. There have also been misses: an imaginative approach to the then two FCs in 1991–92 for support for a merger of the two engineering faculties failed because the FCs could not find a way to collaborate in meeting the (modest) capital requirements; it was an idea 'before its time'. Proposals developed over a number of years for a joint medical school also foundered, as the University of Sussex lost confidence in the idea. However, there have been other benefits: joint courses; and collaboration with local authorities, further education colleges and the local TEC (Sussex Enterprise) on the 'Academic Corridor' project, aimed, among other things, at inward investment and academic 'spin-out' into commerce and industry.

The analysis undertaken by the Joint Planning Group has to be complex and subtle. It depends upon recognition of at least five categories of activity:

- those undertaken by the rest of the HEIs in the UK (not by either the University of Sussex or the University of Brighton);
- those undertaken just by the University of Sussex and other HEIs in the UK (not the University of Brighton);
- those undertaken just by the University of Brighton and other HEIs in the UK (not the University of Sussex);
- those just undertaken by the University of Sussex;
- those just undertaken by the University of Brighton.

From these, permutations of three spheres of activity can be formed for optimum regional effect:

- those in which competition will be encouraged (with ideally a good range of product differentiation);
- those in which joint action is appropriate; and
- those in which each institution will allow the other to pursue the development without direct competition.

As a result the University of Brighton does not intrude upon the heartland of traditional natural science, social science and humanities; its use of these disciplines is almost wholly within an applied and professional context. Meanwhile, the University of Sussex does not have a business school.

Complementarity is hard to achieve, and cuts against many of the instincts of competitive, autonomous institutions and their ambitious managers. The requirements for its successful development and maintenance seem to include the following:

- a good 'fit' of historical patterns of provision;
- relatively 'selfless' governing bodies;
- good chemistry at the chief executive officer (CEO) level;
- a reasonably restricted, or uniform 'reputational' range (so that not all high quality activity is seen in one partner);
- good grass-roots communication between institutional members;
- modest (or realistic) strategic goals;
- the understanding and support of key non-academic partners; and
- at least one high profile joint project.

In the Sussex/Brighton case the last condition is met by the Academic Corridor's 'Innovation Centre'; a classic academic 'incubator' environment as recommended by the Dearing Report (NCIHE 1997: 200). Another example is the success of the Economic and Social Research Council's (ESRC) COPS Centre (Complex Product Systems Innovation Centre), which is the first Research Council centre to be jointly awarded to a 'traditional' and a 'new' university, building on the established reputations of both the Science Policy Research Unit (SPRU) at the University of Sussex and the Centre for Research in Innovation Management (CENTRIM) at the University of Brighton.

Public and private

These dilemmas point up in a stark way the impossibility of answering the question, are universities or colleges in the public or the private sector? In the UK they are both or neither; and they can turn this ambiguity to strategic advantage. They are in fact almost pure exemplars of what have come to be called 'social businesses' or 'organizations which set out to deliver a service of benefit to the community by operating in a business-like fashion' (Pinto 1996).

Richard Whittington has grasped the significance of this in his elaboration of the 'systemic' strategist:

in the Anglo-Saxon world, privatisation and quasi-privatisation have created organisations which must compete, but whose objectives and contexts nevertheless remain much more complex than the simplicities of profit maximisation and perfect markets. The Systemic approach takes these differences seriously. According to the social groups that dominate them, and the immediate social contexts in which they work, businesses vary widely in the ends and means of strategy. To compete and cooperate in this plural environment, we need to be sensitive to the diverse textures of different business systems. Now, more than ever, history and society matter to competitive strategy.

(Whittington 1993: 9)

This is, of course, a very exposed position for managers to occupy (as discussed in Chapter 3). It can often deteriorate as those leading public services come to be identified with the problems rather than the solutions of the domains within which they operate. Higher education leaders, no less than teachers or social workers, walk through the minefield of holding the service together while shouldering blame for its scandals and shortcomings. A recent speech to the Royal Society of Arts (RSA) by Professor Sue Richards neatly caught this dilemma.

Public policy and management have always involved degrees of complexity and uncertainty which even the best private sector managers have found daunting. Stars such as Derek Rayner of Marks and Spencer or Roy Griffiths of Sainsbury's, proposed the remedies of simplification, reining in professional power and discretion and centralizing accountability and responsibility in the hands of budget holders. By now these remedies are part of the everyday life of public policy-makers and managers. For most of the past eighteen years, driven by governments with a desire to spend less of tax-payers' money on public services, public managers have been conscientiously engaged in the pursuit of efficiency, trying in an ever more skilled and capable way to change the ratio between inputs and outputs, delivering efficiency and value for money.

So why do we feel so little like cheering, given this great national success in public management? Part of the answer lies in a prejudice against management which seems to be a prevailing part of our national culture. We still revere professionals rather than management.

(Richards 1997: 31)

Recent publicity for the English RDAs, which the government devoutly wishes to be 'business-led', injects a further level of rhetorical confusion. The 'incorporation' of both polytechnics (in 1989) and colleges of further education (in 1993), along with the slightly earlier formation of NHS trusts, meant a massive increase in the number of formally independent 'businesses' previously unambiguously in the public sector. Directly alongside the chartered universities, these enterprises have to make strategic investment and development decisions, to protect the 'bottom line' of annual budgets and to compete in a variety of market-places. The fact that a significant majority of their contracted activity is with departments of state makes really very little difference. It would, for example, be absurd for the RDA leadership to regard private companies with large government contracts as being in the public sector.

But the gulf remains, despite a parallel trope in official rhetoric worldwide about the value of public–private partnerships. A survey in 1998 by the US National Center for Public Policy and Higher Education revealed, for example, wide differences of opinion between university and business leaders about how their organizations should be run; 64 per cent of business leaders said that higher education should be taking its lead from business (83 per cent believed it should be 'leaner and more efficient'), whereas 77 per cent of college professors said that 'business methods have little use in academe' (Ma 1999).

This US study thus validates the continuing force of an earlier Australian analysis of surveys of strategic planning practices in academic institutions and manufacturing corporations. Noel Kelly and Robin Shaw's reluctant conclusion a decade ago was that:

> academic institutions see corporate planning as a means of resolving problems of internal conflict and resource allocation. They see that such planning is necessary to sequence future activities but they do not attribute to planning any substantive role for the subsequent measurement of performance, in contrast to a major use of corporate planning by corporations.
>
> (Kelly and Shaw 1987: 332)

Optimizing the performance of the college or university, as discussed in Chapter 2, requires overcoming such tendencies by the overlay of a shared sense of institutional purpose and progress, just as major corporations are increasingly sensitive to the positive or negative effects of their internal culture and dynamics.

Reputational positioning

At the end of the day, message-management is fundamentally about both the sector and individual colleges and universities seeking to maintain as much capacity for independent action – as much control over their destinies – as possible. At both levels choices are being made that are fundamentally about positioning. Table 1.2 sets out some of the alternatives in Weberian 'ideal–typical' manner.

No single institution looks like either column in its pure form. The critical issues of strategic choice are, however, the roads not to be followed and the related difficulties of stopping particular activities (so that strategic options become 'substitutional' and not merely 'additive').

If higher education is a 'commodity' it is a very curious one. The major marketing impact is the reputation of the producer rather than that of the product, while other variables that the theory of 'commodification' would require (such as price and specification) are relatively inelastic. As a consequence, maintaining and enhancing a necessarily rather inchoate 'reputation' lies at the heart of strategic planning. It can sometimes prove very fragile, as for example when the highly respected Wesleyan University in Connecticut decided in 1998 (presumably on the basis of professional public relations advice) that it should re-brand itself as the 'Independent Ivy'. The result was a howl of outrage from students, staff and alumni,

Table 1.2   Universities: ancient and modern

Ancient	Modern
Elite	Open
Competitive 'admission'	Accessible 'enrolment'
Full-time	Full-time, part-time, mixed mode
Highly structured	Flexible, modular
Single honours	Many levels, intermediate awards, Credit Accumulation and Transfer Scheme (CATS)
Postgraduate research	Postgraduate and post-experience, continuing professional development (CPD)
Traditional teaching	Innovative learning styles
Subjects and disciplines	Interdisciplinarity
	Professional and vocational applications
Pure/basic research	Applied research, consultancy, 'technology transfer'
Graduates move on to research and further study	High graduate employment
The 'ivory tower'	Many partnerships
National/international reputation	Local/regional role
High costs	High value for money (VFM)

Source: Watson (1998: 77)

and the eventual embarrassment of withdrawal of the slogan (Rolnick 1998).

What this means, as notable higher education strategists have always acknowledged, is that institutions cannot escape their history. It also underlines the values of clarity and distinctiveness, as in the following 'model' example of institutional commitments and drive by the new President of Sarah Lawrence College (a small, but highly regarded, liberal arts college in New York):

> Sarah Lawrence College has something to offer few other colleges do: a dogged belief in the power of the liberal arts to free us; a passionate commitment to a pedagogy focused on serious one-on-one intellectual encounters between faculty and students; a curriculum built on connections among disciplines and on

the interdisciplinary nature of problem-solving and creativity; a lean administrative structure without traditional departments to enhance communication across intellectual boundaries; a vision of the arts as integrated to one another and deeply grounded in the larger liberal arts context.

(Sarah Lawrence 1998)

It is intriguing to compare this passionate statement with the contemporaneous vision and mission statements of four very different UK HEIs.

In publishing its *Strategic Plan 1998–99 to 2202–03*, Cardiff University set out its vision 'to be a world class University' and its mission as follows: 'Cardiff University will pursue research of international excellence and research-led learning and teaching of the highest quality.' Its derivative objectives are four-fold:

- to pursue research of international excellence recognised for its quality and impact on both academic and user communities
- to pursue research-led learning and teaching of the highest quality
- to make a significant contribution to the economic, educational and cultural life of Wales and of Cardiff, and thereby promote the strengths of the region in the UK and the world
- to create an environment in which staff and students can achieve their full potential.

(Cardiff University 1998: 3)

Salford is a 'post-Robbins' creation from a former CAT, an archetype of the institutions most at risk from the DfEE characterization of the pre-1992 universities as 'traditional'. Its 'Strategic Framework' published in 1998, includes six elements:

- to strive for high standards and quality in all areas of activity;
- to recognise the interdependence and equal value of the three core activities (teaching, research, commercial/entrepreneurial activities);
- to have a pro-active attitude towards the changing requirements of society, funders and students; ensuring academic provision is responsive to demand and that students are treated as valued customers;
- to sustain a national and international identity and reputation;
- to identify with the local and regional community, working with others to widen educational opportunities, to secure economic regeneration and to enhance the City of Salford's pride in itself;

- to maintain a commitment to external engagement and partnership with all sectors of society.

(Salford University 1998: 1)

The former polytechnic, Kingston University, has been similarly engaged in re-writing its strategy, using an internal Commission on the Future of Kingston University. This group chose to focus on the areas of teaching and learning, research, recruitment and marketing, lifelong learning, the student experience, management and governance, the portfolio of subjects and local regional and international impact. The resulting draft 'mission' is as follows:

Kingston University seeks to provide a broad spectrum of academic and educational opportunity, reconciling the exploration of ideas with the pursuit of practical skills. It fosters a mutually respectful community, which maximises the potential and fires the imagination of all its members. It strives to be an open listening University, in tune with the life of the locality, while establishing an international presence.

(Kingston University 1998: 1–2)

A rather more functional set of headings structures the 'strategic plan summary' of Edge Hill 'University College', a former public sector College of Higher Education based in Lancashire, which has not yet achieved the degree-awarding powers that, since the Dearing Report, are required for this title. The summary covers 'academic development, students and widening participation, human resources, finance and estates strategy, information and library systems, regional development and partnership' before it issues into the following 'mission statement':

Edge Hill is a major centre of excellence providing a high quality university experience in a responsive learning environment.

Working with a range of partners, and committed to equality of opportunity, Edge Hill provides its students with the knowledge and skills to make key contributions to communities and organisations throughout their lives.

The College's derivative aims are twelve-fold, to:

- achieve continuous improvement in the quality of its provision;
- demonstrate and enhance its commitment to equality of opportunity and, in particular, to improve access for underrepresented groups;

- further improve and continue to make more responsive its service to students and to other customers;
- promote and support the personal development, knowledge, skills and employability of students;
- provide a range of teaching and learning opportunities to support and develop students as autonomous learners;
- promote an institutional culture that encourages and supports scholarship and research;
- promote efficiency and cost-effectiveness;
- develop and maximise the effective use of its human resources;
- develop and strengthen its links with partners in the region to mutual benefit;
- strengthen its image and position in the external marketplace and thereby achieve further increases in the volume and quality of course applications;
- support and contribute to the social, cultural and educational life of local and regional communities;
- develop further international links which reflect diversity and interdependence.

(Edge Hill 1998)

At this stage a cynical reviewer might be tempted to return to Guy Browning's multi-purpose corporate mission quoted in the Introduction. However, close reading of these four texts does identify some more or less clear reputational differentiation.

Thinking in terms of 'universities ancient and modern', an independent observer would find all sorts of declension in these four successive cases: from the unashamed celebration of basic research, through a focus on its applications, to the evocation of 'scholarship'; from international through regional to local; from unqualified pursuit of 'excellence', through the 'broad spectrum of opportunity', to explicit recognition of widened participation. Equally, it is interesting to note the themes struck throughout, in ways that they might not have been a decade ago: the focus on internal staff development and the 'community', the recognition of the geographical context, and the respect paid to teaching (although ironically it is the 'traditional' university that achieves the consistent, politically correct ordering of 'learning and teaching').

2

INTERNAL PERSPECTIVES

Governance and management

What or who, for the purposes of strategic planning, *is* the university or college? In almost all cases in the UK it is the body established by charter or statute as having the supreme responsibility for institutional governance; that is, the Council or Board of Governors. (In a small minority of cases, queried by the Dearing Report, an external Court or Convocation will be the supreme body (Association of Heads of University Administration (AHUA) 1999). There is one vital qualification to this general rule: either through separate establishment or through specific delegation, HEIs will fulfil their responsibilities for academic matters (the curriculum and the confirmation of awards) through a Senate or Academic Board. In almost every case, however, the supreme body will have terms of reference that include a phrase such as 'determining the character and mission' of the institution. In the CUC guide for members, this is set out more prosaically:

> The governing body has a duty to enable the institution to achieve and develop its primary objectives of teaching and research. This responsibility includes considering and approving the institution's strategic plan which sets out the academic aims and objectives of the institution and identifies the financial, physical and staffing strategies necessary to achieve these objectives.
>
> (CUC 1998: 3)

From an international perspective, the Glion Colloquium caught this relationship, and some of the traps into which it has fallen more graphically. After declaring that 'universities have prospered to the extent that they have developed and share an effective and responsive pattern of shared governance', the authors proceed to identify key contemporary tensions:

> This [shared governance] has typically involved a three-fold pattern of public oversight and trusteeship, shared collegial governance and informed – and generally consensual but often short-lived – administrative leadership. Though the particulars have varied with time and place, this overall pattern has proved both durable and effective, but it now shows signs of intense strain. Some public governing bodies have become more politicised than has been historically true, asserting authority over areas once viewed as faculty prerogatives; government ministries and state agencies in some countries have engaged in micromanagement of university affairs; faculty councils have sometimes used their powers to promote special interests, delay action and prevent proposed reforms; administrative leadership has been seen as too weak in some institutions and unwisely assertive in others, while effective management is widely seen as the casualty of these competing interests, held hostage to indecision, compromise and overlapping jurisdiction.
>
> (Glion Colloquium 1998: 7–8)

The relationship between governance (broadly understood, as above) and management will rarely be noticed by the bulk of the university community in a well managed and stable environment. None the less, it is at the heart of the strategic management process. There are several ways in which it can go wrong. Here, for example, is the National Audit Office (NAO) commenting in its *Investigation of Misconduct at Glasgow Caledonian University* on the relationship of the university management to the Court:

> The Council were concerned that, where lay governors are greatly dependent on the executive for information, there is a danger of creating a culture in which the governing body place too much reliance on such information without being in a position to critically evaluate it. In such cases senior management may effectively control the form and content of how issues are presented and limit and restrict any challenge from lay governors.
>
> (NAO 1998: 39)

This judgement was reached in response to what might be termed an extreme situation. However, the HEFCE (not involved with Glasgow

Caledonian) were sufficiently troubled to underline what they meant by 'seek commitment of governing body' in a draft volume of advice on 'appraising investment decisions' in November 1998.

> The decision makers must have an exposition of the business case at an appropriate level of detail to match the scale of the project. It is not sufficient for them to be presented with a 'take it or leave it' decision: they must understand the range of choices open to the institution, and the logic behind the selection of the preferred option.
>
> (HEFCE 1998c: 9)

And the Council will be watching. In describing its own arrangements for audit of the institutions for which it has funding responsibility, it reminds recipients of visits (normally on a three-year cycle) that:

> The HEFCE audit team's involvement with governors inevitably involves discussions about the institution's strategic decision-making process, the quality of information available to the governing body, and the risks associated with particular governance sub-structures.
>
> (HEFCE 1998d: 3)

The Jarratt Committee saw the solution to some of these problems in the establishment of 'hybrid' committees, especially a 'Planning' or 'Planning and Resources' Committee with almost equal numbers of lay Council and elected academic members (CVCP 1985). Most 'traditional' and a small minority of 'new' universities in the UK have these at the end of the twentieth century. But hybridity can bring its own problems, including confusion about management responsibilities and susceptibility to capture by special interest groups.

The Board of Governors at the University of Brighton has described the core relationship between management and governance as one of 'advice and consent'. A statement on corporate governance, widely circulated within the institution, sets this out in more detail:

- The role of the Board, set out in the Articles of Government, is to determine the character and mission of the University, to ensure its solvency and to safeguard its assets. This role is separate from the essential tasks involved in managing the institution. The Board firmly seeks to concentrate on policy development, and to avoid involving itself directly in operational management, for which it holds the Director and senior management responsible. The Board is also sensitive to, and supportive of, the democratic structures of the institution, and gives particular weight to the formal advice of the Academic Board on matters within its sphere of operation.

- This careful division of responsibility depends for its success on a high degree of trust between the Board and the management. The Board expects to receive well formulated policy proposals, and to have access to all background information relevant to those proposals. In practice, the Board expects to work on the principle of 'advise and consent', whereby it debates and refines management proposals, adopts policies, and supports the operational plans devised and implemented by the Director and management team. Where appropriate, however, it takes policy initiatives or makes suggestions and proposals which the management investigates and reports upon.

(University of Brighton 1995: paragraphs 13 and 14)

The planning framework

In the UK, before the advent of the FCs (as a creation of the 1988 Education Reform Act), it was by no means universal practice for institutions to have 'strategic' plans. If they existed, they were created for a particular purpose (for example to put into context external reviews by bodies like the Council for National Academic Awards (CNAA) or the UGC). Alternatively they might have been developed by one of the new breed of vice-chancellors and principals, well imbued with modern management theory, as a way of capturing the attention of less worldly colleagues. Some systematic attention to planning did follow the Jarratt Report in 1985, which talked about bringing 'planning, resource allocation and accountability together into one corporate process linking academic, financial and physical aspects' (cited in Thomas 1996: 34). There was also the influential post-Jarratt textbook, by Geoffrey Lockwood and John Davies (1985). This worked through the implications of what was essentially seen as a defensive move by the CVCP to cope with Department of Education and Science (DES) and political criticisms of drift and lack of accountability (Lockwood and Davies 1985). Meanwhile the so-called public sector had almost all planning taken out of its hands, with the financial control by local authorities and the academic control by the regional Inspectorate (Pratt 1997: 274–88).

Now, however, 'strategic plans' are *de rigueur*, and most institutional planning processes are carefully constructed around what they perceive as Funding Council 'requirements' and what the FCs in turn call 'advice' or 'best practice'. These, for example are the 'ten principles of effective financial management' recently published by the HEFCE to its institutions:

- The governing body is responsible for the direction of, and for the key decisions taken within, the institution.
- The governing body is responsible for the financial health of the institution.
- Roles and responsibilities of the governing body, all committees, the head of the institution and senior managers should be defined, understood, accepted and reviewed regularly.
- The competencies of the governing body, all committees, the head of the institution and senior managers should satisfy the institution's needs and should be reviewed regularly.
- The institution should plan strategically.
- There should be a corporate plan which includes a financial strategy as one of its major components.
- Opportunities and risks should be recognised, assessed and managed.
- Information to governors, the head of the institution and senior managers should be relevant, reliable and timely.
- Communication should be effective throughout the institution.
- Structures, processes and systems should be in place which are robust and fit for purpose.

(HEFCE 1998e: 6–7)

Later on, the same document unpacks the recommended procedures for meeting these requirements, including those of strategic or 'corporate' planning (HEFCE 1998e: 18–21). It is no accident that the HEFCE's most systematic advice about strategic planning should be expressed within a financial context, since it is, of course, money and a purchaser–provider contract that structures the key relationships between institutions and the Council. However, as indicated in the last chapter, the Funding Council has its own mission to pursue and external 'direction' to satisfy, and these will not be fulfilled just by buying student numbers.

This is where the philosophy of institutional autonomy can become tricky and the vocabulary and grammar more than a little weaselly. All of the FCs, since their foundation in 1988, have 'received' strategic plans and, initially, almost entirely independent five-year financial forecasts. In consultation document 98/13 the HEFCE proposed:

to introduce a three-year collection cycle for corporate plans which would include a financial strategy. The focus for monitoring and review would be the strategic messages in these documents. In the course of the three-year cycle, we would ask for some additional policy or business strategies to inform policy development and funding initiatives. Each summer we would collect staff and student forecasts, the financial forecast, and an annual operating plan.

(HEFCE 1998f: 1)

The remainder of the document hints at what these additional 'policy or business strategies' might include: 'learning and teaching; access and widening participation; interaction with business and the community; research' (HEFCE, 1998f: 3).

According to Circular Letter 3/99, the sector broadly concurred, with 95 per cent of respondents agreeing that corporate plans should be collected by the Council on a three-year cycle, and 82 per cent agreeing that the Council should revive its former practice of collecting 'annual operating statements' as part of an annual return. The Council was also able to declare almost universal acquiescence in the core elements to be included in the corporate plan, as follows:

- the mission/vision;
- major external and internal factors likely to impact upon the institution;
- the current strategic position of the institution;
- long-term aims;
- principal objectives;
- financial strategy underpinning the corporate strategy; and
- main proposals for implementation and associated measurable targets.

(HEFCE 1999b)

Simultaneously, the thematic shopping list was revised as 'priority areas where additional funding will be made available in order to support development and innovation across the sector, and *which we expect to be relevant to all institutions*' (emphasis added). There was also the hint that systematic compliance could reduce transaction costs by supplying the necessary background for a 'single annual exercise' of bidding for HEFC special funding. Of the themes, learning and teaching, and widening participation survived, as did business and the community through the Council's new 'Higher Education Reach Out to Industry and the Community' programme. However, they were joined by 'growth and restructuring an institution's student numbers and subject provision' (principally through the manipulation of additional student numbers, and presumably to aid convergence on sector-wide funding norms for teaching), 'effective estate management' (now including 'improving the capital infrastructure'), 'developing information strategies', and 'recognizing and encouraging good management of HEIs' (on which a new initiative is promised). Research dropped off the list, no doubt temporarily (HEFCE, 1999b).

In its circular at the end of this process, the Council not only confirmed its intention to implement Circular Letter 3/99, but also noted its intention to deploy its team of regional consultants to discuss with 'their' institutions the following 'themes':

- recognising and encouraging excellence in teaching and learning;
- widening student access and participation;
- encouraging HEIs to apply their expertise and facilities in working with business and the wider community;
- supporting growth and restructuring in institutions' student numbers;
- effective estate management and improving the capital infrastructure;
- developing information strategies; and
- recognising and encouraging good management of HEIs, including effective financial management, human resource management and strategic planning.

(HEFCE 1999c: 2)

These headings thus join a long list of strategies, policies and plans, which, from the internal perspective are all *required* by outside bodies. They thereby join the 'inescapable agenda' discussed above (p. 31). A contemporary list is set out in Table 2.1 (by source) and Table 2.2 (by topic).

The topics listed are, of course, in addition to audit requirements for subsidiary companies, public policy on such matters as the PFI, restrictions on loan finance, requirements of the Charity Commissioners applying to endowment income, tax strategies (including VAT planning), and the host of other obligations of large, complex organizations at the end of the twentieth century. Satirical heads of institutions ponder how long it will be before the HEFCE estates department offers guidance on the academic application of Feng Shui. From the perspective of the university or college, making sense of this sea of advice, exhortation and expectation poses some special challenges.

Table 2.1 Summary of external requirements and advice for HEIs in England: sources

Source	Requirements and advice
Association for University and College Counselling (AUCC)	**Student welfare** *Degrees of Disturbance: The New Agenda. The impact of increasing levels of psychological disturbance among students in Higher Education*, March 1999.
Beachcroft Wansbroughs Solicitors	**Student litigation** *Student Litigation – Avoiding the Risks*, August 1999.
British Universities Finance Directors Group (BUFDG) Accounting Standards Group	**Annual accounts** (see also HEFCE; CVCP/COSHEP/SCOP) *Accounting in Higher Education Institutions*, March 1995. *Technical Update*, June 1997.
Chartered Institute of Public Finance and Accountancy (CIPFA)	**Treasury management** (see also HEFCE) *Treasury Management in Higher Education: A Guide*, 1995.
Commission on University Career Opportunity (CUCO)	**Childcare** *Childcare in Universities and Colleges*, January 1996. **Flexible working** *Flexible Working in Universities and Higher Education Colleges*, April 1997. **Equality** (see also CRE/EOC/CVCP) *Equality Targets Action Planning and Monitoring in Universities and Colleges*, January 1996. **Recruitment, selection and promotion** *Recruitment, Selection and Promotion for Universities and Colleges in Higher Education*, November 1997. **Disability** (see also DfEE; HEFCE) *Guidelines on Disability for Universities and Colleges in Higher Education*, October 1997.

Table 2.1 (*cont'd*)

Source	Requirements and advice
	Harassment *Guidelines on Harassment for Universities and Colleges in Higher Education,* April 1999.
Commission for Racial Equality (CRE)/Equal Opportunities Commission (EOC)/Committee of Vice-Chancellors and Principals (CVCP)	**Equal opportunities** (see also HEFCE; QAAHE) *Higher Education and Equality: A Guide,* June 1997.
Committee of University Chairmen (CUC)	**Governance/whistleblowing** *Guide for Members of Governing Bodies of Universities and Colleges in England, Wales and Northern Ireland.* Ref 98/12, March 1998.
Committee of Vice-Chancellors and Principals (CVCP)	**'Free speech' and extremism** *Extremism and Intolerance on Campus.* Management Guide, July 1998. **Sport** *Sport in Higher Education.* Task Force Report, December 1996. **Skills in the curriculum** *Skills Development in Higher Education,* November 1998. (CVCP/DfEE/HEQE) **Student discipline** *Student Disciplinary Procedures Notes of Guidance,* December 1994. **Student appeals and complaints** *Independent Review of Student Appeals and Complaints,* April 1998. **Meningitis** *Managing Meningitis in Higher Education Institutions.* Management Guide, June 1998. **Drugs and alcohol** *Guidelines on Drugs and Alcohol Policies for Higher Education.* Management Guide, June 1997.

Table 2.1 (*cont'd*)

Source	Requirements and advice
	Health and safety of students *Health and Safety Guidance for the Placement of HE Students*. Management Guide, March 1997.
	Estates (see also HEFCE; NAO) *Procurement Guidelines for Higher Education: Building and Engineering Projects*. Management Guide, January 1997.
	International students *Recruitment and Support of International Students in UK Higher Education*. Management Guide, October 1996.
	Town and country planning *Guidelines on Town & Country Planning*, Parts 1–18, 1995–1996.
	Purchasing (see also HEFCE; NAO; JPPSG) *Purchasing Performance Appraisal*. Management Guide, December 1995. *Purchasing in Higher Education – A Directory (Third Edition)*. Management Guide, March 1997.
	Revaluation of estates *Revaluation 1995 – Memorandum of Agreement, CVCP, SCOP*. June 1996.
	Course advertising *Guidelines for Good Practice in Purchase and Management of Course Advertising*, February 1995. *Guidelines for Good Practice in Course Advertising*, February 1995. *Course Advertising – Key Questions*, February 1995.
	Access and widening participation *From Elitism to Inclusion: Good Practice in Widening Access to Higher Education*, November 1998 (with HEFCE, SHEFC, SCOP, COSHEP, CIHE).

Table 2.1   (*cont'd*)

Source	Requirements and advice
CVCP Research Careers Initiative	**Contract research staff** *Employing Contract Researchers: A Guide to Best Practice*, October 1998.
Committee of Vice-Chancellors and Principals (CVCP)/ Committee of Scottish Higher Education Principals (COSHEP)/Standing Committee of Principals (SCOP)	**Accounts** (see also BUFDG; HEFCE) *Statement of Recommended Practice: Accounting in Higher Education Institutions,* July 1994.
Council for Industry and Higher Education (CIHE)	**Employability** *Helping Students Towards Success at Work: An Intent Being Fulfilled*, September 1998 (with CVCP/CBI).
Department for Education and Employment (DfEE)	**Free speech (1986)** *Education No. 2 Act, 1986.*
	Disability Statement (1997) (see also CUCO; HEFCE) Disability Discrimination Act 1995. *Disability Discrimination Act 1995, Code of Practice – Rights of Access – Goods, Facilities, Services and Premises, 1999.*
	Private Finance Initiative (PFI) (see also HEFCE) *Exploring PFI Options in Education and Employment – A Guide for Decision Makers,* March 1996.
Department of the Environment, Transport and the Regions (DETR)	**Environmental strategy** *Sustainable Development – The UK Strategy*, 1994. (DoE). *Environmental Responsibility – A Review of the 1993 Toyne Report*, 1996 (DETR, with Ali Khan). *The Government Environmental Education Strategy*, 1996.
	Environmental management *Environmental Management Systems: A Guide for the HE Sector*, 1998 (DETR, with Forum for the Future).

Table 2.1 (*cont'd*)

Source	Requirements and advice
Education Counselling Service (ECS) (British Council)	**Overseas marketing** *Draft Code of Professional Standards and Ethics for ECS Subscribing Institutions*, 1999.
European Union	**European policy statement** *SOCRATES VADEMECUM*, 1995 (European Commission (EC)).
	European environmental policy *Towards Sustainability: A European Community Programme of Policy and Action in Relation to the Environment and Sustainable Development* (also called the *Fifth Action* Programme), 1992 (European Commission).
Health and Safety Executive (HSE)	**Health and safety** *Health and Safety Management in Higher and Further Education: Guidance on Inspection, Monitoring and Auditing*, 1992.
Higher Education Funding Council for England (HEFCE)	**Corporate plans** *Institutions' Corporate Plans*. Consultation 98/13, March 1998.
	Audit Code of Practice *Audit Code of Practice*. Report 98/28, June 1998.
	Financial strategy *Effective Financial Management in Higher Education. A Guide for Governors, Heads of Institution and Senior Managers*. Report 98/29, June 1998. *Strategy for Costing and Pricing. Application for Funds*. Invitation 98/32, June 1998. *1998 Planning Return and Financial Forecasts*. Request 98/27, May 1998. *Appraising Investment Decisions. Draft for Consultation*. Consultation 98/55, October 1998.
	Financial memorandum *Model Financial Memorandum Between the HEFCE and Institutions (Revised)*. Circular C15/97, July 1997.

Table 2.1 (*cont'd*)

Source	Requirements and advice
	Treasury management (see also CIPFA) *Treasury Management Value for Money – National Report.* M12/96, May 1996. *Treasury Management Study in the Higher Education Sector – Management Review Guide.* M13/96, May 1996. *The Financial Health of Higher Education Institutions: A Report of Good Practice.* M16/95, September 1995.
	Private Finance Initiative (PFI) (see also DfEE) *Private Finance Panel: Guidance on PFI Projects.* Circular Letter 6/97, April 1997. *A Step-by-Step Guide to the PFI Procurement Process.* Circular Letter 22/97, August 1997. *Practical Guide to PFI for Higher Education Institutions.* Good Practice 97/28, November 1997. *Practical Guide to PFI for Higher Education Institutions (Revised).* Guide 98/69, November 1998.
	Accounting (see also BUFDG; CVCP/COSHEP/SCOP) *Accounts Direction for Academic Year 1996–97.* Circular Letter 37/96, December 1996.
	Access and widening participation (see also CVCP) *Widening Participation in Higher Education: Funding Proposals.* Consultation 98/39, August 1998. *Widening Participation: Special Funding Programme 1998–99.* Invitation 98/35, June 1998.
	Research *Research Activity Survey 1997.* Request 97/21, October 1997. *Research Assessment Exercise 2001: Key Decisions and Issues for Further Consultation.* RAE 1/98, July 1998.

Table 2.1 (*cont'd*)

Source	Requirements and advice
	Learning and teaching *HE2005+ Towards a Sectoral Strategy for Teaching and Learning in HEIs.* M17/96, May 1996. *Learning and Teaching: Strategy and Funding Proposals.* Consultation 98/40, August 1998. *Guidelines for Accessible Courseware.* Guide 99/05, February 1999. *Learning and Teaching: Strategy and Funding.* Report 99/26, April 1999. *Institutional Learning and Teaching Strategies: A Guide to Good Practice.* Good Practice 99/55, September 1999.
	Interaction with the business community *Institutions' Corporate Plans.* Consultation 98/13, March 1998.
	Estates strategy (see also CVCP; NAO) *Strategic Estate Management.* Circular 1/93, 1993.
	Maintenance investment plan *Strategic Estate Management.* Circular 1/93, 1993. *Building Repairs and Maintenance Study in the Higher Education Sector: National Report.* 98/30, June 1998. *Building Repairs and Maintenance Study in the Higher Education Sector.* Management Review Guide, 98/31, June 1998.
	Disability (see also CUCO; DfEE) *Proposed Specification for Disability Statements to be required from Institutions.* Consultation Paper CP3/95, December 1995. *Specification for Disability Statements Required from Institutions.* Circular 8/96, May 1996. *Disability Statements. A Guide to Good Practice.* Guide 98/66, November 1998. *Guidance on Base-level Provision for Disabled Students in Higher Education Institutions.* Guide 99/04, January 1999.

Table 2.1   (*cont'd*)

Source	Requirements and advice
	Purchasing (see also CVCP; NAO; JPPSG) *Procurement Strategy for Higher Education.* M26/96, September 1996. **Energy policy** *Energy Management Study in the Higher Education Sector: National Report.* M5/96, February 1996. *Energy Management Study in the Higher Education Sector: Management Review Guide.* M13/96, May 1996. **Equal opportunities** (see also QAAHE; CRE/EOC/CVCP) *Policy Statement on Equal Opportunities in Quality Assessment.* M 2/96, February 1996. **International activity** *Guiding Principles for International Activity.* Circular Letter 8/99, March 1999. **Cultural and sports facilities** *Partners and Providers. The Role of HEIs in the Provision of Cultural and Sports Facilities to the Wider Public.* Report 99/25, April 1999. **Indirectly funded partnerships** *Higher Education in Further Education Colleges: Code of Practice on Indirectly Funded Partnerships.* Consultation 99/37, June 1999.
Higher Education Funding Council for England (HEFCE) Joint Information Systems Committee (JISC)	**Information strategy** *Guidelines for Developing an Information Strategy,* December 1995.
Higher Education Funding Council for England (HEFCE) National Audit Office (NAO)	**Purchasing** (see also CVCP; HEFCE; JPPSG) *University Purchasing in England,* May 1993.

Table 2.1 (*cont'd*)

Source	Requirements and advice
Higher Education Funding Council for England (HEFCE)/ Scottish Higher Education Funding Council (SHEFC)/ Higher Education Funding Council for Wales (HEFCW)/ Department of Education Northern Ireland (DENI)	**Information systems and technology management** *Information Systems and Technology Management Value for Money Study.* Management Review Guide 98/43, September 1998. *Information Systems and Technology Management Value for Money Study.* National Report 98/42, September 1998.
Higher Education Statistics Agency (HESA)	*HESA Circular 94/22* (December 1994) covers the main requirements by the agency of institutions, as follows: **Student data** *Individualized Student Record/Aggregate Record of Non-credit-bearing Courses/First Destinations* **Staff data** *Staff Individualized Record/Research Output Record/Staff Load Return* **Finance data** *Finance Statistics Return/Estates Record*
Joint Costing and Pricing Steering Group (JCPSG)	**Costing and pricing** (see also JPPSG) *Integrating Financial and Academic Decision Making: Strategy for Costing and Pricing,* May 1999. *Costing and Pricing for Decision Makers in Higher Education: User Guide,* May 1999.
Joint Procurement Policy and Strategy Group (JPPSG)	**Purchasing** (see also CVCP; HEFCE; NAO) *Procurement Strategy for Higher Education,* September 1996. *Procurement Benchmarking for Higher Education,* September 1997. *Equipment Purchasing,* August 1998. **Costing** (see also JCPSG) *Whole Life Costing: A Good Practice Guide for End Users and all those Involved in the Procurement Process,* September 1998.

Table 2.1 (*cont'd*)

Source	Requirements and advice
National Audit Office (NAO)	**Estates** (See also CVCP; HEFCE) *The Management of Building Projects at English Higher Education Institutions,* January 1998.
Quality Assurance Agency For Higher Education (QAAHE)/ Higher Education Quality Council (HEQC)	**Quality assurance** *The Quality Assurance Code of Practice: Students with Disabilities.* Draft Report, July 1999 (QAAHE). *Code of Practice for the Assurance of Academic Quality and Standards in Higher Education. Section 2: Collaborative Provision,* July 1999 (QAAHE). *Guidelines on the Quality Assurance of Distance Learning,* 1999 (QAAHE). *Quality Assurance in UK Higher Education: A Brief Guide,* 1998 (QAAHE). *Guidelines on the Quality Assurance of Research Degrees (the Research Degree Guidelines),* 1996 (HEQC). *A Quality Assurance Framework for Guidance and Learner Support in Higher Education: The Guidelines,* 1995 (HEQC). *Guidelines on the Quality Assurance of Credit-Based Learning (the Credit Guidelines),* 1995 (HEQC). **Quality assurance and overseas institutions** *Code of Practice for Overseas Collaborative Provision in Higher Education,* 1996 (HEQC).
United Kingdom Education and Research Networking Association (UKERNA)	**Internet services** *JANET Acceptable Use Policy,* April 1995.
Universities and Colleges Employers Association (UCEA)/ Universities Safety Association (USA)	**Stress** *Dealing with Stress in Higher Education: How to Get Started.* Management guidance, June 1999.

Table 2.2 Summary of external requirements and advice for HEIs in England: topics

Access and widening participation	HEFCE; CVCP/HEFCE/SHEFC/ HEFCW/SCOP/COSHEP/CIHE
Accounting	BUFDG; HEFCE; CVCP/COSHEP/SCOP
Advertising of courses	CVCP
Audit code of practice	HEFCE
Business community (interaction with)	HEFCE
Childcare	CUCO
Contract research staff	CVCP Research Careers Initiative
Corporate plans	HEFCE
Costing and pricing	JPPSG; JCPSG
Cultural and sports facilities	HEFCE
Disability	CUCO; DfEE; HEFCE; QAAHE
Drugs and alcohol	CVCP
Employability	CIHE/CVCP/CBI
Energy policy	HEFCE
Environmental management	DETR
Environmental strategy	DoE; DETR
Equal opportunities	CUCO; CRE/EOC/CVCP; HEFCE
Estates	CVCP; NAO
Estates strategy	HEFCE
European environmental policy	EC
European policy statement	EC
Extremism on campus	CVCP
Finance data	HESA
Financial memorandum	HEFCE
Financial strategy	HEFCE
Flexible working	CUCO
Free speech	CVCP; DfEE
Governance/whistleblowing	CUC
Harassment	CUCO
Health and safety	HSE
Health and safety of students	CVCP
Indirectly funded partnerships	HEFCE
Information strategy	HEFCE/JISC
Information systems and technology management	HEFCE/SHEFC/HEFCW/DENI

Table 2.2 (*cont'd*)

International students	CVCP
International activity	HEFCE
Internet services	UKERNA
Learning and teaching	HEFCE
Maintenance investment plan	HEFCE
Meningitis	CVCP
Overseas marketing	ECS
Private Finance Initiative (PFI)	DfEE; HEFCE
Purchasing	CVCP; HEFCE; HEFCE/NAO; JPPSG
Quality assurance	QAAHE; HEQC
Quality assurance and overseas institutions	HEQC
Recruitment, selection and promotion	CUCO
Research	HEFCE
Skills in the curriculum	CVCP/DfEE/HEQE
Sport	CVCP
Staff data	HESA
Stress	UCEA/USA
Student appeals and complaints	CVCP
Student data	HESA
Student disciplinary procedures	CVCP
Student litigation	Beachcroft Wansbroughs Solicitors
Student welfare	AUCC
Town and country planning	CVCP
Treasury management	CIPFA; HEFCE

The first is simply that of priority and authority. Buried in here are statutory requirements, contractual commitments and 'conditions of funding' that will force them to the top of any list of management tasks and make them unavoidable pegs in the ground of the institution's annual cycle. That said, the resulting cycle may not itself be fully rational (it does, after all, have multiple sources and multiple authors) and there will be scope for the system to be flexed to institutional advantage. Equally, the trap must be avoided of only responding to the potential external 'sticks', thereby missing some of the 'carrots' and also failing to extract what is of real, high priority importance to the institution's core mission and business.

The HEFCE shows its own understanding of a hierarchy of priorities. In a guide on 'how the HEFCE promotes value for money', it segregates: 'benchmarking' (which aims to give institutions the information to assess their own 'performance'); 'best practice guides' (which 'enable universities and colleges to establish general principles that will help all institutions reach the standards of the best, both within the sector and outside'); 'value for money studies' (which 'go a stage further than best practice guides by identifying and quantifying the service improvements and savings that can be achieved'); and 'case studies' (to 'show how principles of best practice have been applied and the lessons to be learned') (HEFCE 1998g: 3–4). In measuring a reaction, it is valuable to keep these distinctions in mind, not least by recognizing that the paymaster has his own funding source (the DfEE, and behind it the Treasury) breathing down his neck and requiring both accountability and value for money.

An associated challenge is to understand and respond effectively to the rhetoric, and to the market-place, that the ocean of advice represents. Nearly all of these documents state that responsibility for their particular area should be taken 'at the highest level', that 'senior management commitment' is an essential prerequisite for progress, or that formal institutional endorsement and adherence is the only way forward. Their authors will not have taken account of the fact that they themselves are competing for senior management time, or that there is the danger of the perverse outcome of formal response without internalized recognition of the implications. An acid test is how often the university or college returns to review the policies (on equal opportunities, or on environmental responsibility, for example) that it is shamed or enthused into initially adopting.

These two challenges – of scanning and prioritizing, and of placing the material in the institutional context – lead inevitably to a third: making decisions about the distribution and devolution of both responsibility and resources. There are clearly no fixed answers to these questions. Central and local responsibilities will sensibly vary from institution (according to size, organizational philosophy and mission) and possibly also over time. Robert Shirley has helpfully identified four basic levels at which 'decision issues' arise and can be resolved within HEIs: that of 'institutional strategy' (like 'basic mission'); that of 'campus-wide functional strategy' (addressing the 'how' questions for 'total institution in a systematic way'); 'program strategies' (developed and owned by schools and departments, however constrained by the former two levels); and 'program-level functional strategies' (identifying particular action steps) (Shirley 1983). The main drive should be for the organization as a whole to understand the pattern that has been chosen, what is being done in its corporate name by all of its constituent parts, and equally important to be able to review and reassign these expectations as circumstances change.

Continuity and change

Many of the areas listed above represent responses to new or changed circumstances. Others (like those on 'value for money' or procurement of major projects) are about the FCs in particular passing on, or at least seeking to share responsibility for meeting public obligations. The institution has to ride with all of these currents and waves, and remain true to itself.

This implies, critically, establishing the right balance between continuity and change. A much underrated institutional value is that of 'steadiness', of identifying and nurturing a set of core commitments while seeking to adapt them where necessary to meet changed circumstances. Only by ensuring such steadiness (and the predictability that goes along with it) can institutions like universities and colleges ride out waves of often short-term contextual pressure and maintain the confidence of those who have invested, who are investing, and who might in future invest in their enterprise. As the leading US commentator puts the point in his recent comparative study of five European institutions, *Creating Entrepreneurial Universities*, 'effective collective entrepreneurship does not carry a university beyond the boundaries of academic legitimacy, setting off a downmarket cycle of reputation, resources and development' (Clark 1998: 4–5).

Two contrasting cautionary tales of the 1990s underline this essential strategic truth.

The first is the fate of Thames Valley University (TVU), a creation of the late 1980s' drive for first polytechnic and then university status, and widely regarded as in the vanguard of a new, accessible, flexible and above all socially responsible higher education. The Thames Valley mission is bravely unambiguous:

> TVU supports mass participation in higher education as a contribution to equality and social justice, and is committed primarily to teaching and learning and playing a major part in the educational, cultural and economic life of the region. It supports these policies by developing and sustaining partnerships

with other organisations and providers in the public, private and voluntary sectors.

In November 1998 much of this ambition fell apart (many will hope temporarily) as a highly critical QAA report indicated that the university was in 'a position where its academic standards and the quality of its students' experience were and are under threat and can only be maintained by special measures' (QAA 1998a). A mixture of rapid and apparently insufficiently embedded change, endemic trade union hostility to management (which precipitated the key crisis, as teachers refused to complete assessments in the summer of 1997), and recruitment and related financial uncertainty, led to the resignation of a charismatic vice-chancellor, the exposure of inadequate other senior and middle management and the arrival of the commissioners in the form of a renowned vice-chancellarian troubleshooter and an experienced consultant as his deputy. Neither those sections of the press keenly hostile to the purposes and achievements of mass higher education nor the trade union at the centre of the controversy was slow to dance on the grave (Clare 1998; Halpin 1998; HEFCE 1998h; NATFHE 1998).

The full QAA report – sent to the library of every UK HEI, presumably as a cautionary tale – underlines some of the perceived structural weaknesses leading to the outcomes described above: lack of preparation for significant academic restructuring; associated errors of judgement about the extent to which major changes in academic programmes required systematic review and revalidation; both compounded by simultaneous administrative reorganization and a very high level of turnover among the university's most senior staff. In these circumstances the impact of industrial action, confusion about the roles and responsibilities of committees and groups reporting to the Academic Board, and isolated misjudgements about such matters as the motivation and ability of applicants as well as the proper response to the concerns of external examiners, proved finally explosive. Most damning of all was the auditors' conclusion that 'the university has lacked any period of stability' (QAA 1998b: 14).

The 'upside' contrast to this story is the rise of another 'new' university, this time of the post-Robbins variety, as the University of Warwick enters the new Millennium cast as the 'entrepreneurial' university setting the standard for those 'post-Baker' institutions with ambitions in this direction, and thereby overcoming its own trade union-inspired opposition to management decisions of the late 1960s (Thompson 1970).

Visitors to the university's web-site in early 1999 will find a page dedicated to hyperbolic 'press quotes [*sic*] about Warwick', of which the first is typical: 'Warwick University ... its stellar performance in research, its brilliance at generating income and its joining the unofficial British Ivy League. It is now the BMW of the university world' (*Independent*, 14 May 1998). Clark's study shows where this reputation, and the performance that backs it up, has come from in its just over 30 years of institutional life. His thesis centres on five 'pathways of development' or 'common transforming elements' in the chosen case studies:

- a 'strengthened steering core' (which must 'operationally reconcile new management values with traditional academic ones');
- an 'expanded developmental periphery' (bringing 'into the university the project orientation of outsiders');
- a 'diversified funding base' (springing critically 'discretionary funds for internal investment');
- a 'stimulated academic heartland' (in the 'entrepreneurial university the heartland must adopt a modified belief system'); and
- an 'integrated entrepreneurial culture' (in other words, a 'work culture that embraces change').

(Clark 1998: 3–8)

The substantive account of Warwick's developmental trajectory includes not only the early rocky period alluded to above, and its key response to the Conservative government's cuts of the early 1980s (the 'earned income policy' that led, among other things to the renowned Warwick Manufacturing Group, an internationally orientated business school, the Warwick Science Park, and its well deserved lead in the university based conference trade), but also a string of more contemporary innovations (such as the Graduate School and appointment in 1995 of 36 founding Warwick Research Fellows). In terms of the application of Clark's 'pathways', features that deserve underlining are: the strong strategic control from the centre (from the committee system and in particular the Star Chamber-like 'Earned Income Group' – Clark goes so far as to say that in these circumstances the 'university can be entrepreneurial without the vice-chancellor necessarily being entrepreneurial'!); the critical role of planned cross-subsidy; and perhaps most crucially, that the 'Warwick phenomenon' did not occur overnight (Clark 1998: 11–38).

In so far as there is a single moral in these contrasting stories, it is surely about maintaining an acceptable balance (or indeed an acceptable tension) between elements of continuity and elements of change, especially as they relate to the values of the institution as understood by its members. Mark Easterby-Smith concludes a study of change and innovation in higher education with the stark conclusion that 'it is the values of staff and students that can be the greatest source of, and barrier to, change and innovation':

> Senior managers get easily excited at the possibilities of being able to 'manage' the values of their organisations. But this is much more difficult than the popular textbooks would have us believe, and very dangerous. The danger is that if one simply attacks the existing values of an organisation – say those of scholarship, colleagueship and individual freedom – one runs the risk of destroying individuals' sense of purpose and thus creating a highly demoralised institution. If values are to be shifted, say towards a greater commercial orientation – then they must be done in such a way which allows for retention of the original ideas in parallel. It is a kind of bridging idea which is needed. This will take time, and not a little creativity.
>
> (Easterby-Smith 1987: 51)

Optimizing the operation

Chapter 15 of the Dearing Report, *Higher Education in the Learning Society* focused directly on the management and governance of institutions (NCIHE 1997: 228–47). It is one of the parts of the report that has received strongest condemnation from within the sector (see for example Shattock, 1998). Equally it is one of the parts of the report with which external stakeholders are apparently most comfortable (CIHE 1997). This tension is easily explicable: the Dearing Committee was determined to follow through the logic of council/board responsibility for strategy (as set out above) and also to see public ownership by these bodies of the outcomes. In doing so, they ran the risk of treading on the toes of both Senates/Academic Boards and the college or university managers.

The device chosen was that of the periodic review. Paragraph 15.54 begins by reiterating that 'the performance of an institution is at the centre of a governing body's responsibility.' It goes on to acknowledge the strength of the arrangements that underpin this in a financial sense: 'a powerful regulatory framework is already in place through the financial memorandum between the institutions and the funding bodies and a range of audit requirements, with which a governing body must comply.' But this will not be enough:

> we believe that it is necessary to recommend a new and stronger focus within institutions, in which governors periodically review

the performance of the governing body and the institution across a wider spectrum than that captured by the current regulatory framework. Institutions should put in place an all-embracing and systematic review, involving the senate or academic board, so that, over a five year period, the following strategic matters are reviewed:

- a participation strategy which addresses participation by those under-represented in the institution;
- a re-assessment of the staff development strategy;
- determining and reassessing a formal framework for engaging with external constituencies;
- the size of the governing body and its effectiveness for decision-making;
- arrangements for making academic awards in the institution's name.

(NCIHE 1997: 242)

A page later this emerges into a fully fledged 'recommendation' with the additional provisos that, firstly, 'the outcomes of the review should be published in an institution's annual report' and, secondly, that 'the Funding Bodies should make such a review a condition of public funding' (NCIHE 1997: 243). It was, of course, the latter proviso that sent a chill into university leaders' hearts, and it is interesting that the government has apparently backed off this suggestion (see the analysis in Chapter 1 of *Higher Education for the 21st Century* (DfEE 1998b)).

The kind of institutional research or institutional 'self-study' that generates information for systematic review of strategy and policy is much more common in the USA than in the UK, and indeed often a significant item of investment for the college or university (Chan 1993). A key issue is how to achieve objective analysis not only of the impact of the whole (as in the 'reputational positioning' analysis mooted in Chapter 1) but also the sum of the parts.

Here institutional culture impacts in a peculiar way. Not only can 'local' managers fall prey to self-satisfaction (whereby all their geese are swans), but the loyalties to existing patterns of provision make it hard to release the resources for genuinely new and radical developments. There is also the trap of commissioning, and then ignoring, the compilation of huge amounts of data. The Cornell economist Ronald Ehrenberg has prepared a witty and persuasive account of the inapplicability of his professional training to the problems of running his university. Discussing the allocation of space (the most contentious faculty based issue after car-parking in the modern HEI), he declares that he 'followed the dictum of the provost, who while a musicologist often thought more like an economist than [he] did, that if information is not going to be used, don't bother to incur the costs of collecting it' (Ehrenberg 1999: 114).

Andrew Bruce suggests that in the business world 'all too often internal resources are confused with real sources of sustainable advantage.' He proposes a three-point test for the evaluation of initiatives, which, with a little adaptation to the academic environment (substitute 'student' or 'sponsor' for 'customer' and 'teaching and research' for 'product and service'), could produce some helpful guidance:

- Firstly, they must provide product and service attributes that are valued by their customers (whether internal or external).
- Secondly, these product and service attributes must be provided at a level of performance that is superior to the competitors in the eyes of the customers.
- Thirdly, this superiority of performance must be sustainable through modification of the resource when required.

(Bruce 1999: 9)

The time-honoured device for such analysis is the SWOT ('strengths, weaknesses, opportunities, and threats') matrix, ideally at the level of the individual course or subjects. Quite sophisticated variants have been constructed, including a very influential model from John Sizer (now chief executive of the SHEFC). Sizer's approach proceeds along two axes, scoring as high, medium or low aspects of (internally driven) relevant institutional strength and (externally driven) 'subject area attractiveness'. The aim is to spring a series of management actions from (most favourably) endorsing growth to (least favourably) 'planned withdrawal and redeployment' (Sizer 1982).

The trick appears to be that of keeping an eye on the whole as well as the laborious sum of the parts. In this sense the 'reality check' incorporated in the QAA criteria and indicators for 'university status' set out in Table 2.3 provides a demanding template.

In many ways this listing is a counsel of perfection. One, more pragmatic, way of reading it is as identifying the range of levers available for managing strategic decision making. How confident, for example, is the institution about not only identifying and supporting the good new idea that will improve its economy and reputation, but also the not-so-good idea that will drain time, energy and other resources? Similarly, the well founded institutional strategy will also help to identify the time when a formerly good idea has exhausted its shelf-life.

Table 2.3   University status: QAA criteria

Criteria	Evidence
A Governance and management	
(a) The institution's governance, management, financial control and quality assurance arrangements are sufficient to manage existing operations and respond to development and change	The institution should be able to demonstrate that: • its academic and financial planning, quality assurance and resource allocation policies are coherent and relate to its mission, aims and objectives; • there is a clarity of function and responsibility in relation to its governance and management systems; • across the full range of its activities, there is demonstrable depth and strength of academic leadership; • policies and systems are developed, implemented and communicated in collaboration with staff and students; • its mission and associated policies and systems are understood, accepted and actively applied by staff and, where appropriate, students; • it is managing successfully the responsibilities vested in it pursuant to the grant of degree awarding powers, or by its validating university; • its operational policies and systems are monitored, and that it identifies where, when, why and how changes might need to be made; • there is demonstrable information to indicate continued confidence and stability over an extended period of time in its governance, financial control and quality assurance arrangements, and organizational structure.
B Quality assurance	
(a) The institution has clear and consistently applied mechanisms for establishing its academic objectives and outcomes	The institution should be able to demonstrate that: • its programmes of study are offered at levels that correspond to the levels of the overall qualifications framework for higher education;

Table 2.3   (*cont'd*)

Criteria	*Evidence*
	• in seeking to establish, and then maintain, comparability of standards with other providers of equivalent level programmes, advice is explicitly sought from academic peers in other higher education institutions and, where appropriate, professional and statutory bodies.
(b) The institution seeks to ensure that its programmes of study consistently meet stated objectives and outcomes	The institution should be able to demonstrate that: • self-assessment is integral to quality assurance and the management of the institution; • ideas and expertise from within and outside the institution, on programme design and development, on teaching, and on student learning and assessment, are drawn into its arrangements for programme approval and review; • staff are informed of, and provided with guidance on, its policy and procedures for programme design, monitoring and review; • its strategies for teaching, learning and assessment relate to its stated objectives and learning outcomes; • there is a close interrelationship between academic planning matters and decisions on resource allocation.
(c) Programme performance is carefully and regularly monitored	The institution should be able to demonstrate that: • responsibility for amending/improving new programme proposals is clearly assigned and subsequent action carefully monitored; • close linkages are maintained between learning support services and programme approval, planning and review; • clear mechanisms exist for assigning and discharging action in the scrutiny, monitoring and review of existing programmes;

Table 2.3 (*cont'd*)

Criteria	Evidence
	• coherence of programmes with multiple elements or alternative pathways is secured and maintained; • clear mechanisms are employed when a decision is taken to close a programme or programme element, and, in doing so, the interests of students are safeguarded.
(d) The effectiveness of the institution's learning and teaching infrastructure is carefully monitored	The institution should be able to demonstrate that: • the effectiveness of teaching and learning is monitored in relation to stated objectives and learning outcomes; • collections of books and other materials contained in, or directly accessible through, its library/learning resources centre are adequate to facilitate the programmes pursued by students in the institution; • action is taken to maintain and enhance quality and the role of staff and students in this process; • students are advised about, and inducted into, programmes and study, and account is taken of different students' needs; • means exist for identifying good and poor practice and for disseminating and implementing improved operational methodologies.
(e) The academic and related support requirements of students studying off-site are taken into account	The institution should be able to demonstrate that: • clear and understood arrangements exist for monitoring the opportunities and achievements of those of its students studying outside the institution, including those outside the UK.
(f) Standards of students' achievements are maintained at a recognized level and there is a strategy for	The institution should be able to demonstrate that: • through its assessment practices, it seeks to define, monitor and maintain its academic standards;

Table 2.3 (*cont'd*)

Criteria	Evidence
developing the quality of academic provision	• its assessment criteria and practices are communicated clearly to students and staff; • it assures itself that its assessment practices fully cover all declared learning objectives and learning outcomes; • external peers are engaged in its assessment processes; • consistency is maintained between internal and external examiners' marking; • the reliability and validity of its assessment procedures are monitored and that its assessment outcomes inform future programme and student planning; • students are informed of the outcomes of their assessment; • information on assessment outcomes is given to students in a timely manner; • constructive feedback is given to students on their performance.
(g) Effective action is taken to address weaknesses, promote strengths and demonstrate accountability	The institution should be able to demonstrate that: • a rigorous approach is adopted in response to matters raised through self-assessment; • actions are regularly monitored to ensure the maintenance of quality and standards; • feedback from students, staff and external interest groups is secured and evaluated and clear mechanisms exist to provide feedback to interested stakeholders; • use is made of feedback at departmental, programme or programme-element level; • external views and involvement are sought in programme design and review, teaching and student learning; • information arising from feedback is disseminated within programmes and across the institution;

Table 2.3   (*cont'd*)

Criteria	*Evidence*
	• the effectiveness of student advisory and counselling services is monitored and resource demands arising from such activities are considered and acted upon; • effective means exist for encouraging the continuous improvement of quality of provision and student achievement.
C Administrative systems (a) The institution's administrative systems are sufficient to manage its operations now and in the foreseeable future	The institution should be able to demonstrate that: • its administrative support systems are able to monitor student progression and performance and provide timely and accurate information to satisfy academic and non-academic information needs; • it provides access to comprehensive library and computing services, support and demand for which is regularly monitored and, where appropriate, improved; • high quality and confidential support services are provided for students and staff; • equality of opportunity is achieved in its activities; • it has in place effective and confidential mechanisms to deal with all complaints regarding academic and non-academic matters; • its administrative staff are given adequate opportunities for professional development.
D The environment supporting the award of higher degrees (a) The institution has an environment of academic staff, postgraduates and postdoctoral workers	The institution should be able to demonstrate that: • it exercises prudent management of its portfolio of research and consultancy activities;

Table 2.3 (*cont'd*)

Criteria	Evidence
which fosters and actively supports creative research and scholarly activity	• a substantial proportion of its academic staff are engaged in research and scholarship; • in the majority of academic areas within which it undertakes research, or other forms of advanced scholarship consistent with its mission, it demonstrates achievement of national and/or international standing; • it is successful in securing income for its research activities; • it has implemented effectively the provisions of the QAA Code of Practice on Postgraduate Research programmes.

E Academic staffing

  (a) The qualities and competencies of staff are appropriate for an institution with university title

The institution should be able to demonstrate that a significant proportion of its academic staff have:
• higher degrees, doctorates, relevant professional qualifications and fellowship of learned societies;
• teaching and/or research experience in other universities in the UK and abroad;
• experience of curriculum development, assessment design and research management in other universities and HEIs;
• relevant experience outside higher education, for example in professional practice or in industrial research and development.

  (b) The institution's staff are actively engaged with the pedagogic development of their discipline

The institution should be able to demonstrate that:
• a significant proportion of its academic staff are active in subject associations, learned societies and relevant professional bodies;
• a significant proportion of its academic staff participate in professional development schemes;
• there are institutional and local-level strategies of staff development designed to establish, develop and enhance staff competences;

Table 2.3 (*cont'd*)

Criteria	Evidence
	• an extensive portfolio of teaching development activities has been established.
(c) Staff of the institution have acknowledged academic expertise	The institution should be able to demonstrate: • that a significant proportion of its academic staff are engaged in research, academic reviews and scholarly commentary, and produce articles, text books and other academic-related materials; • that it has academic staff who are invited to contribute to the work of expert committees, as advisers, expert witnesses or commentators; • that it is able to attract individual or institutional commissioned research and/or consultancy; • the extent to which it is able to attract funding or sponsorship for academic development initiatives; • that it is valued as a partner in collaborative projects; • that it is involved in research partnerships and technology transfer schemes with outside enterprises.
(d) Staff maintain high professional standards and willingly accept the professional responsibilities associated with operating in a university environment	The institution should be able to demonstrate that: • feedback on performance is regularly received from students, employers and other institutional stakeholders; • the outcomes of external scrutiny exercises undertaken by bodies such as the QAAHE, the FCs and professional and statutory bodies are carefully considered and actioned; • a significant proportion of its staff act as external examiners in other higher education institutions; • a number of its academic staff act as external academic auditors, external subject reviewers, or in some other external review capacity.

Source: Based on QAA 1999: 23–9

Ensuring satisfaction

Sound strategy, of course, implies not only well founded directional and investment choices, but also retrospective and recurrent performance monitoring and evaluation. Here the current fashion is the prioritization of client satisfaction. 'Clients' come in different shapes and sizes, and with differing interests

First and foremost there are *students*, whose personal investment in both participation and success continues inexorably to increase. Although collectively they have recently proved more passive in the UK than either their predecessors of earlier generations or their current international contemporaries, there is growing evidence of their sensitivity to the quality of their experience, and its value in the economic and social context. Student views are characteristically gathered through course questionnaires and direct feedback, and their academic interests are still safeguarded by the external examiner system. There have, however, been more imaginative and general approaches, such as that pioneered at the University of Central England, which builds upon 'student satisfaction' as a proxy for quality (Harvey *et al.* 1997).

Lee Harvey is one of several designers of student opinion instruments who have come to stress the importance of the completion of an 'action cycle'. In his words, 'there should be a clear idea of what information is being collected, what sort of decisions it will affect and how the information will help to implement change'. All too often the 'feed-back loop' is not closed, and students are left unaware of how and to what extent their analysis has effected change (Harvey 1999).

A related problem is leading the witness, or at least assuming that you know what he or she is going to say. An extensive survey of part-time students at the University of Brighton in 1998 was expected by academic staff to confirm their view of the weakness of environmental and support services for such students. A parallel survey of staff produced two clusters of points for most serious attention in the interests of their students: 'standard of teaching and other accommodation and general ambience' and 'availability of catering facilities'. In the event; these top two features were relegated by the students to positions 11 and 24 respectively: their top cluster – by a clear margin – was 'improved academic support and feedback on assignments and progression' (University of Brighton 1999).

The simplistic temptation, especially now that most students in the system are not on full-time first degrees, and that most of those are technically 'mature' (over 21 on entry), is to tackle this issue by regarding students as 'customers', and hence to be satisfied by the straightforward application of 'customer care'. But this apparent simplicity breaks down in practice. Not only can student consumers not simply purchase their degrees (or return them if they are unhappy), but most students (and especially those who have paid considerable fees themselves, for example for professional postgraduate and post-experience courses) continue stubbornly not to regard the fundamental transaction as financial. They are at least as keen to be 'members' as 'customers' of 'their' institutions, and to play a full part in its deliberative and strategic development.

This complexity links with a variety of *sponsors*, now backing students at all levels. To the traditional parental and familial means of support have now been added the institutions themselves (as providers of scholarships and other financial assistance), the state (through payment of fees and providers of maintenance support for a group of its future employees) and other employees (including through such new devices as the 'golden hello'). Collectively, their sensitivity to costs and value for money may be higher, but in general their concerns about the quality of the experience of those they sponsor also loom large. This is probably the group with which institutions have been least likely to canvass opinion.

Employers more generally have their organized means of expressing opinions about higher education, as set out at the beginning of this chapter. Wise institutions, however, build up tailor-made subsets of these groups (on a geographical or functional basis) to assist their development of departmental and institutional strategy. Time-honoured mechanisms include 'industrial advisory boards' as well as the use of individuals as members of committees or examiners, or on appointment panels. The precision with which messages are solicited, understood or acted upon is, however, very variable, as recent studies of the extent to which institutions make genuine use of labour market information (LMI) would appear to confirm (DfEE 1998g, 1998h).

Finally, it is important to remember that *staff* are also in key respects clients of the institution, dependent upon it for their own career progression and satisfaction as well as providing the frame within which they can develop and promote their individual and group achievements. The late discovery in the history of university and college strategic plans of the 'staff development' and the 'human resource' categories is evidence of increasing sensitivity to this point (Knight and Harvey 1999).

Academic staff (sometimes termed 'faculty' in traditional universities) are, of course, the creators and guardians of the institutional cultures described in the Introduction. But they can also be members of trade unions and professional bodies seeking to improve their position through collective bargaining. They can also be occasionally cruelly dismissive of the interests of other categories of staff, whose positive influence on the learning experience of students and on the efficient conduct of research is increasingly recognized. As a leading administrator writes:

> Modern-day administrators, even at relatively junior levels, play a full part in the enterprise of higher education. They are not just the rule-keepers but increasingly the rule-shapers; they are closely involved in many academic initiatives and will, through wide knowledge of external agencies, government policies and financial possibilities, together with a deep understanding of, and support for, the institution's ethos, help to steer their university on a sound strategic course. Administrators have an increasing knowledge of business and management concepts and are applying these, where appropriate, to the running of higher education. They see administration as a profession they are proud of and they expect career progression and personal development during their work.
>
> (Thorley 1998: x)

Balancing these voices and interests is a key management challenge. So is maintaining communication with them all. One of the most often repeated complaints about those offering feedback and advice to HEIs is the feeling that it goes into a black hole, never to re-emerge. At least as much effort in communicating feedback on feedback as goes into its initial generation is well worth the investment.

Whatever the state of art of monitoring and evaluation, both lead inevitably to sector-wide performance indicators, and these in turn lead inexorably to league tables, where the journalistic desire to build whole-sector rankings out of whole-institution composites of scores on various criteria has led to some predictable outcomes. For the institutions these vary between public triumphalism (by the winners – much though they may deprecate the methodology in private with their less successful peers) and angry despair by the losers (whose 'missions' they claim have been cruelly distorted by unfair and inappropriate tests).

The objections are of two main kinds: empirical and theoretical (or, more strictly, methodological). The first argues that secure national statistics, on such sensitive matters as 'drop-out' (complicated as this is by the tendency of the new higher education to encourage variable pace of study, intermediate qualifications, course and credit transfer and all the other trappings of genuine life-long learning) do not (yet) exist. More sophisticated critics are also inclined to rely on the categorical mistake made in turning measures into goals and targets (Goodhart's law was developed to warn the Bank of England that 'as soon as the government attempts to regulate any particular set of financial assets, these become unreliable as indicators of economic trends'; I am indebted to Professor Michael McIntyre for its broader description: 'when a measure becomes a target, it ceases to be a good measure').

The second objection rails against the distortions caused (some suggest wilfully) by the choice, weighting and, above all, the combination of various statistics (Berry 1999). 'Quality' is a case in point where the lead has been taken by one newspaper (*Daily Telegraph*) in equating a quality assessment score of 22/24 points with 'excellence', thereby not only riding roughshod over the QAA (and formerly the Funding Council) insistence that these scores are in any case criterion-referenced, but also disregarding all other lower scores (including some poor scores in other subjects by the emerging high-flyers). Similarly, 'new' universities resent the historical bias associated with research-related scores, as well as the apparently 'anti-access' implications of a focus on entry grades. Weighting such matters highly automatically leaves them at the foot of the overall table, even though on some key indicators associated more directly with their professional and vocational missions – especially employment upon graduation – they do distinctively well as a group. Meanwhile the overall effect of combination is (as in schools league tables) to emphasize relative prosperity. The message seems to be that academic performance is directly related to inherited wealth or penury.

However, no amount of collective or individual cries of 'foul' will make these exercises go away, as (perhaps largely because of the institutions' historical failure to make such a deficit good in other ways) the public undoubtedly see them as an essential element of the system's transparency. In the USA this public appetite is now allied with a more widespread acceptance by the institutions that league tables are a fact of life; this is, of course, eased by the fact that there are so many of such tables (most colleges or universities can underline their missions by appearing reasonably high on at least one). Certainly the fear, frequently expressed here, that league tables lead to homogeneity of mission is not borne out by the US case. United Kingdom institutions will have to keep their nerve, continue to press collectively for methodological improvements, but also work individually to improve in and then publicize their success against the indicators that matter most to them.

There have been several attempts at 'internal' (that is, by the sector) leadership of the performance indicator debate. None has yet met with widespread endorsement; indeed several groups have simply given up. The latest initiative, coordinated by the FCs, is that of the Performance Indicators Steering Group (PISG). Their first report summarizes progress towards output measures of performance relating to:

- learning and teaching of students;
- extension of knowledge through research;
- application of the knowledge and resources of higher education to the needs of business and of society more generally.

(HEFCE 1999d: 1)

For the first measure, the relevant indicators are listed as: access, progression, 'outcomes', efficiency and employability. For the third, attention is directed to the value of industrial contracts, the turnover of higher education companies, income from licences and options, and from software. Much ingenuity is directed towards avoiding unsatisfactory comparisons and rankings (by, for example, the intention to provide for each institutional outcome a set of 'context statistics' derived from 'comparable institutions'). (HEFCE 1999d: 6, 8, 25). However, early responses do not give much confidence of a positive outcome. Among the thorny problems still unresolved are the reduction of teaching 'efficiency' back to a full-time norm, and the disregard of value for money in research.

'Wicked' issues

However rational and well understood the institutional strategy may be, this does not prevent the emergence, and the intransigence of certain issues, which it cannot apparently resolve. Social policy experts term these 'wicked' problems, for which there is no logical or consensual solution. The seminal formulation comes from what is now a classic article in planning theory:

The search for scientific bases for confronting problems of social policy is bound to fail, because of the nature of those problems. They are 'wicked' problems, whereas science has developed to deal with 'tame' problems. Policy problems cannot be definitively described. Moreover, in a pluralistic society there is nothing like the indisputable public good; there is no objective definition of equity; policies that respond to social problems cannot be meaningfully correct or false; and it makes no sense to talk

about 'optimal solutions to social problems' unless severe qualifications are imposed first. Even worse, there are no 'solutions'
in the sense of definitive and objective answers.

(Rittel and Webber 1973: 155)

Other disciplinary perspectives are also relevant. Philosophers like
Alasdair MacIntyre worry about public loss of confidence in their
profession if moral dilemmas in contemporary culture appear to be
insoluble. MacIntyre writes about 'a salient and continuing feature
of academic philosophy, of which those outside academia are often
very well aware', namely 'the large inability of professional academic philosophers to arrive at agreed solutions to their own central
problems and the corresponding apparent lack of substantive progress
within philosophy'. The key example is that of moral disagreement:

Hence, it is unsurprising that to some people at least the moral
life appears as pervasively problematic, a source of recurring
dilemmas, while others avoid dilemmas by invoking some particular highly determinate moral scheme, but only at the cost of
equally recurrent contention both with those who uphold some
rival and incompatible scheme, and those who oscillate between
one position and another. So it is with disputes about abortion.
So it is over issues of distributive justice and the morality of
war. So it is on occasions when the claims of truthfulness compete with those of responsibility for the well-being of others or
of oneself or of the state.

(MacIntyre 1993: 66)

Meanwhile, Sir Isaiah Berlin saw his most important contribution
to social theory as the thesis that 'fundamental ethical and political
values are so diverse and conflicting that societies must make choices
among them that inevitably sacrifice some important values to others'
(Berlin 1969: 118–72).

One set of such 'wicked issues' is shared by universities and colleges
with all large and complex employers in the late twentieth century.
These include car-parking, tobacco-smoking and security, especially
personal security. The problems as well as their solutions move on
broadly in step. Thus, the advent of environmentally responsible
policies of charging for on-site car-parking has led to disputes with
neighbours when employees choose to clog up adjacent streets, while
the health-conscious non-smoking policies of large organizations
have led to the ubiquitous phenomenon of huddles of addicts clus-
tered around entrances to buildings. Simultaneously, those sites with
multiple entrances in urban neighbourhoods have found their policies

of open access threatened by the incursion of drug-users, against whom the latest tactic is the installation of ultra-violet ('blue') lighting in ground-floor lavatories. A common feature of this set of problems is that they are all basically 'hygiene' factors.

Of the above, stress is probably the issue that arouses the most heat and generates the least light. It is, for example, the staff issue most likely to be identified as uniquely problematic in whichever sector, sub-sector or organization is under scrutiny. Yet after musculoskeletal disorders (affecting approximately 1.2 million people in work in 1995), it is the second highest cause of reported illness ('stress, depression or anxiety' at 279,000) (HSE 1998: 13). In many sectors – especially the public service in general, and education and higher education in particular – it is associated with perceived loss of personal professional control and the 'new managerialism' alluded to in the Introduction (for example, Fisher 1994). It has also inspired a backlash, as some psychologists, as well as the predictable management gurus claim that 'stress is a natural phenomenon . . . without it nothing would get done' (Lacey 1998; Gwyther 1999). (For a balanced 'managerial' response to these dilemmas see Grier and Johns 1998.)

There are also common features to this 'public sector' list of issues. Several (such as league tables) stress accountability for public funding, and a concomitant interest in comparative performance (at least as much directed at 'naming and shaming' the weak as praising and setting up for emulation the strong). Others (like pay) emphasize perceived under-funding for core services, as well as (in the era of 'public – private partnerships') lack of a clear strategy for capital investment. Probably most palpable, however, is the provider's sense of 'rationing': that there is greater demand for services than can be supplied, and that the price of greater or more democratic access is a threat to quality, of having to do more with less.

Another distinct higher education set of issues arises from the special position of students (especially younger students) as members of the institution: from noise in the neighbourhood, and the incidence of drug use (including cannabis in halls of residence), to the kind of prurient publicity attracted by stories such as the recent (rarely verified) wave of headlines about student prostitution (Aaronovitch 1998; Gibson 1998; Hodges 1998). 'Life-style' issues pose particular problems for HEIs, as old fashioned notions of *in loco parentis* are now well and truly buried, and the institutions compete for the custom of increasingly worldly wise and sophisticated school-leavers. Prospectuses, videos and other promotional material now stress the entertainment services of university and college towns and cities, and in more than one instance can be said to have gone over the top. In 1999, for example, Liverpool John Moores University was widely accused of endorsing a 'Club 18–30' image of undergraduate life (Robertson 1999).

There are also more serious concerns about the psychological pressures on students, as well as evidence about their increased vulnerability to mental health problems. An admittedly incomplete survey of student suicides conducted by the office of the Liberal Democratic Education spokesman showed these to have increased from 2.4 in every 100,000 of the student population in 1983–84 to 9.7 in 1993–94 (AUCC 1999: 31).

Without going over the top in this way, HEIs have to adapt to the reality that the traditional notion of a student life apart from the stresses and strains of society, or in Michael Oakeshott's famous phrase 'a gift of an interval', is now a thing of the past. Serial studies of the financial circumstances at the University of Brighton demonstrate not only the erosion of resistance to debt and significant increases in the amount of paid work undertaken during term time, but also interesting consumption choices. In 1998, 39 per cent of second year students reported having debts of over £1000, compared with 28 per cent in 1996, 20 per cent in 1994 and 13 per cent in 1992. Meanwhile uptake of student loans increased from 40 per cent in 1992 to 43 per cent in 1994, 56 per cent in 1996 and 68 per cent in 1998. Regular employment in term time went up from 27 per cent in 1992 to 46 per cent in 1998 (with 39 per cent of those working undertaking more than 15 hours per week in 1998). However, 47 per cent of a not particularly wealthy student population owned or had regular use of a car and 66 per cent a computer. Nor is this just a feature of an older student population: the figures for car and computer ownership of those under 26 were 40 per cent and 64 per cent respectively (Kular and Winn 1998: 43, 45–7).

These controversies highlight the fact that universities and colleges are in almost all cases places where people live as well as work, and wish to derive additional benefits from living together. The fact that they are voluntary communities, and almost invariably more heterogeneous than the host society that surrounds them is another source of on the one hand strength and opportunity and on the other threat and tension. The presumption of toleration – of, for example, differences in faith, in sexual orientation, in nationality, and especially in political allegiance – is central. So too is the existence and application of policies such as equal opportunities and freedom from harassment. In this connection it is interesting that a recent survey by the Inter-faith Network of the United Kingdom concluded that 'institutions with secular foundations that aim for an inclusive approach to religious life on campus appear to be the most successful at accommodating the needs of different faith groups' (Gilliat-Ray 1999: vi).

Membership of such a community implies, of course, submission to a degree of collective self-regulation, and not just in academic matters. Universities and colleges need to be able to enforce an appropriate type of discipline, to deal with complaints and grievances and generally to regulate their affairs. But they cannot and should not expect to stand apart from the civil and criminal law of the country. This was the boundary mapped out on behalf of the CVCP by the Zellick Report of 1994, although it focused exclusively on student discipline (Zellick 1994). Zellick's principle, of basic deferral to state procedures, has, almost inevitably, been subsequently criticized from both sides: from those not willing to see any alternative to public procedures, and those (especially feminist critics – it is relevant that the case leading up to the Zellick inquiry was one of alleged sexual assault) who see university processes as potentially filling in dangerous gaps in the application of the law.

Many of the Zellick Group's difficult disciplinary issues, including for example that of potential double jeopardy, apply equally to staff. Another that directly connects the interests of staff and students is that of consensual sexual relations, where an unresolved argument rumbles on about whether the asymmetry of the power relationship between tutor and pupil can ever safely be set aside to respond to physical attraction (Billinghurst 1995; Bristow 1995; Charter 1995). Trade unions and professional associations have had periodic initiatives designed to agree upon a code of practice, and one UK university (Bradford) has taken unilateral action by way of a 'registration' procedure rather than a ban, but have so far been defeated by a persuasive minority of their members (Swain 1999).

A further set of community based dilemmas forms the subject matter of a hard-hitting report from the Home Office-funded Police Research Group, entitled *Policing the Campus* (Campbell and Bryceland 1998). The authors begin by unpacking the informal pattern of collusion between the police force and university and college authorities to minimize the reporting of incidents: the former to protect clean-up rates and the latter to prevent unfortunate publicity. (In the USA 'sunshine laws' and the federal Student Right to Know and Campus Security Act of 1990 have made such subterfuge illegal.) They then demonstrate that campuses are at least as vulnerable to general patterns of crime, such as burglary and housebreaking, theft and car crime as the wider community. Meanwhile, detailed investigation (based in part on the criminological literature and in part on their survey of university officers) shows the probability of a significantly higher incidence of drug and alcohol misuse among young people in further and higher education than in their contemporaries elsewhere. In this respect it is fascinating finally to note the almost identical rank order of personal risk factors reported by university and police officers, as follows (in decreasing order of significance):

- physical characteristics of the campus (for example, isolated buildings, remote car-parks, poor lighting);
- location of the campus (for example, inner city, rural);
- alcohol/drug misuse;
- relationship of the campus to the surrounding community (for example, 'town and gown' conflict);
- physical characteristics of staff and students (for example, age and gender);
- racism.

(Campbell and Bryceland 1998: 13, 17, 43, 60–6)

The report concludes with a predictable set of recommendations on improving partnerships, adopting multi-agency approaches to drug and alcohol abuse, and improving design for security, but its main achievement is to highlight the special and often intractable problems of the campus. The authors almost understate their case by describing HEIs as 'in effect small communities in their own right with a population equal to and in some senses greater than housing estates and small villages' (Campbell and Bryceland 1998: 1). By the time you add in the pathologies of staff and other players, I prefer the characterization of Don Aitkin, the vice-chancellor of the University of Canberra: 'I sometimes refer to my own university as an Italian Renaissance town of 10,000 souls, extraordinarily creative, effervescent and productive, but occasionally inclined to lapse into backstreet brawls and character assassination' (Aitkin 1998: 122).

How such problems are approached – even if they cannot be made to go away – will say a lot about the fundamental mission and character of an institution. But there are some moral and meta-physical battlegrounds that are peculiar to higher education as a whole. A tough case, on which much progress has been made, with the willing cooperation of enlightened staff, is the use of animals in experimentation and research in disciplinary areas like medicine, pharmacy and biology. Of the perennial issues, the most central and strategically vital, is freedom of speech and its professional variant, usually summarized as 'academic freedom'.

Higher education communities are fundamentally committed to the notion of academic freedom, in the sense of the ability of their members to follow ideas, including uncomfortable ideas wherever they may lead. However, this commitment also implies an obligation to enter into dialogue about such ideas and their implications (Dworkin 1996). In other words, and to use the analogy of the American Constitution, a type of 'first amendment' freedom – to speak out and to hold controversial views – has become perverted into a kind of 'fifth amendment' defence (silence to prevent self-incrimination). Such a battle was fought out over the terrain of external, peer quality review, resulting in the uneasy compromise of the QAA in the late 1990s (Watson 1995). However, two more specific controversies served to bring this commitment and its boundaries into public and political discourse in the mid-1980s.

The first was the Conservative government's new funding system, and the fear that it could lead to an external funder constraining intellectual activity within an individual institution. This led to safeguards being added to the 1988 Education Reform Act in the House of Lords, to reduce the powers of the government and the FCs as its agents from making funding decisions that impacted on individual institutions.

The second arose from the frustration of the same government with the use by student unions of so-called 'no-platform' policies, especially to deny right-wing spokespersons access to student audiences. This led to the specific requirement in the Education (No. 2) Act of 1986 that institutions, and specifically their student unions, 'take such steps as are reasonably practical to ensure that freedom of speech within the law is secured for members, students and employees of the establishment and for visiting speakers' (CVCP 1998c: 14–15).

Linked with freedom of speech, and often seen as a dangerous reciprocal to freedom of expression is the tendency, much more advanced in the USA, to devise codes of speech and practice to avoid offence. The derogatory term of art for these is 'political correctness', which has sprung a series of libertarian assaults within the academy on some soft liberal assumptions (Rauch 1993).

A final controversy, also shared by other major public services, is the drive (following scandals of maladministration mainly in the health service, but with some echoes in university life) to protect the interests of employees 'speaking out', at risk to their own careers. This has led both the CUC and the CVCP to advise institutions to create their own 'whistle-blowing' codes of practice and procedures (CUC 1998: 39). Following this trend, the *Times Higher Education Supplement* has established its own weekly 'Whistleblowers' column, although after a few months very few genuinely 'new' cases have come to light. The column has also had to own up to the fact that one of its star witnesses took out no fewer than 15 industrial tribunals against a variety of employers in a period of 18 months; all were unsuccessful (THES 1998: 6). There is the concomitant danger, identified by commentators on US politics (where whistle-blowing has had some of its most spectacular effects) that too early and too earnest recourse to the public podium can result in a dramatic break-down of trust and of civility (Klein 1998).

Management approaches to apparently insoluble issues generally fall into three categories. There is the 'fire-fighting' approach, often coupled with a propensity not to deal with the problem until it has become a crisis. This has some apparent advantages: it seems to ration management effort; it tackles the problem 'just in time'; and anyway, according to the legendary principle of 'unripe time', it might just go away. On the downside, it does allow matters to get worse, and the problems concerned tend to repeat themselves. Then there are the 'strenuous interventionists', concerned to be seen to take all such issues seriously. They run straight into the common feature of 'wicked' issues: that there are just not enough resources to put the root causes right. As a result the core problems endlessly re-cycle and management impotence becomes more and more apparent. Thirdly, there are the 'reflective pragmatists', who attempt to apply their and the institution's values calmly and methodically.

In acknowledging that 'wicked problems' do not have 'an enumerable (or an exhaustively describable) set of potential solutions', the authors of the concept come close to endorsing this third way:

> In such fields of ill-defined problems and hence ill-definable solutions, the set of feasible plans of action relies on realistic judgment, the capacity to appraise 'exotic' ideas and on the amount of trust and credibility between planner and clientele that will lead to the conclusion, 'OK let's try that'.
>
> (Rittel and Webber 1973: 164)

Judgement is of the essence here, and often one good has to be allowed to trump another (see the discussion of 'emotional intelligence' in Chapter 3). The result is inevitable disaffection in some quarters, but choices are seen to be made, energy is spread sensibly and explanations can be made to the community. Such pragmatists elect to do least harm, to avoid zealotry, and progressively to disengage from unsatisfactory practice. They are also particularly good at spotting 'proxy' battles, when protagonists of extreme points of view are really fighting for other forms of redress. Most importantly they achieve the peculiarly 'academic' requirement of leading by enabling. In the face of yet another 'wicked issue' they can be relied upon to take the sensible and least destructive next step.

The 'strategic plan': *desiderata*

From the account above of both external and internal pressures, requirements and opportunities, it should by now be clear that managing strategy is not just about producing a plan; it is even more about managing a process, or, more accurately a series of processes. It is only through an interlocking series of sub-strategies, policies and arrangements for their monitoring and evaluation that anything like *strategy* on an institutional or corporate scale emerges.

To follow the logic of the preceding section, the key operational sub-strategies appear to be those relating to:

- learning and teaching;
- research and 'knowledge exchange' of various kinds (including intellectual property rights (IPR));
- human resources (including staff development);
- information management;
- marketing and promotion; and
- estates development.

Some of these map directly on to external requirements like the UK FCs' long-standing insistence on estates strategies and more recent discovery of learning and teaching. Others are much more susceptible to local customization.

In carrying forward a joint project on estates statistics, the four UK FCs identify four 'core concerns and objectives' as follows:

- meeting organizational needs (including delivering the strategic plan objectives);
- managing costs effectively;
- utilizing space efficiently;
- managing the estate well (that is, continuing to 'improve and create value').

These are then linked with a series of 14 'key estates ratios', for which it is intended to produce sector-wide benchmarks (HEFCE 1999e: 8). Some of the early results are dramatic, for example the identification of 31 per cent of institutional space as 'requiring major repair or inoperable' (HEFCE 1999e: iv). Reaction to such 'median' data must, however, be locally determined, with confidence in some cases, about the reasons for an individual institution to buck the trend.

The approach to learning and teaching is necessarily more open-ended. Here, for example, is the list of components of a learning and teaching strategy, considered by an HEFCE Task Force on the issue in 1998–99:

- An analysis of the problem or context facing the institution that the strategy addresses (e.g. student numbers, student diversity, funding, changes in employment context);
- Statements of a goal or vision (e.g. to increase access, to support more diverse students, to move from a teaching-centred to a learning-centred approach, to develop postgraduate training, to achieve high TQA scores);
- Learning and teaching tactics that are anticipated to be adopted (e.g. the adoption of more resource-based learning, more communication and information technologies, more collaborative learning, adoption of an outcomes-based curriculum);
- Mechanisms that will be adopted to help bring about the desired changes (e.g. reward of excellent teachers, new systems of student feedback, course evaluation or review, policy on requirements for ILT accreditation for new and experienced teachers, provision for funding teaching development projects, creating a learning resources centre);
- Means of managing the implementation and monitoring the impact of the strategy (e.g. quality assurance procedures, a Learning and Teaching Committee overseeing a schedule with targets for each component, an Evaluation Office, new requirements in annual departmental reporting).

(HEFCE unpublished; see also HEFCE 1999f)

The same balance of external and internal drivers is true of the overarching institutional policies which should inform both strategy and practice. These will almost invariably include the following:

- equalities (including disability);
- environmental responsibility (including such things as energy use and transport);
- financial policies (including treasury management);
- international policy; and
- widening access (once voluntary, now required).

So what should an overall strategic plan include, for both external and internal consumption? There is a worked example in the Appendix, available for real-world critique. The analysis so far suggests, however, that it must carefully balance:

- a 'mission' that is as distinctive as possible;
- a set of 'goals' that are realistic, but also 'stretching' in the right directions, and are above all understandable by those responsible for helping to meet them;

- a set of operational plans, including assigned responsibilities and targets;
- a coherent fit between the programmes and plans of the macrocosm (the college or university) and the microcosm (its constituent parts – faculties, schools, departments and the like); but above all
- a statement of values, against which both concrete and most abstract progress (for example, the quality of the community) can be tested.

Finally, it is useful to reflect on the kind of things a well formed strategic plan should assist a management team to do, or how it will aid decision making. Some of the issues here are simply tactical (like deciding whether or not to bid for Funding Council or government initiatives, or which external partnerships would really add value to the operation). Others go to the heart of the academic community itself (like making the case for cross-subsidy of less by more prosperous areas, or making space for new developments by winding down other activity). A third, and increasingly important set is about identity and self-image: once academics and their supporters were centrally exercised by the question 'what is a university (or college)?'; now they are much more likely to have to respond effectively and coherently to the question 'what sort of university (or college) are you?'

The sector's favoured responses to such questions have all too frequently been characterized by a simplistic appeal to diversity, often as means of evading more searching questions about distinctive mission choice and reputational positioning. One possible future is that the system settles on a number of 'key types' or 'essential species'. I have attempted elsewhere to enumerate these as they appear to be emerging within the British system:

- the international research university;
- the modern professional formation university;
- the 'curriculum innovation' university;
- the distance/open-learning university;
- the university college;
- the specialized/single-subject college (Watson 1999: 333).

This kind of analysis is, of course, as heuristic and as unempirical as that in Table 1.2. It does, however, underline the importance of a sense of a centre of gravity within institutional strategic thinking. It also exposes the dangers of trying to win in all of the varied markets for higher education, against any kind of odds, and all of the time.

3

PERSONAL PERSPECTIVES

Preparing for strategic management

The chief executive of a college or university, along with his or her most senior team, is directly responsible in most governance schemes for analysing and proposing strategy to the institution's policy making body (the Council or Board of Governors), and then, once agreed, for carrying it out. Given the complexity, ambiguity and above all the potential role conflict implied in facing upwards and outwards as well as downwards and inwards, why – apart from the drive for status and (much more recently) material reward – would anyone want to take on such a job? Why not, for example, remain part of the academic community (from which the vast majority of such post-holders still come) from which the view upwards can remain satisfyingly cynical and acerbic? Here is 'Prinny' from Sussex again, musing on his (or her?) long wait during the spring and summer of 1998, for a replacement vice-chancellor:

> Friends trapped within the Sussex House bunker (the University's administrative HQ) tell me that they can 'barely stay awake' with excitement over the appointment of a new Vice-Chancellor. An advertisement, headed 'Smart Boy Wanted', has been placed in the window of the Post Office in the Refectory, and informs us that the actual work for finding Professor Charming has been given to a temping agency. Even more extraordinary – it seems that the agency is looking for suggestions, cutting down on the effort required in order to nab that fee, which can be sent to them by popping a name on a piece of paper, putting it in a bottle and lobbing it off the end of the Palace Pier. The University has

the opportunity to appoint someone who would lead from the front, armed with clear ideas, prepared to face up to the future. I fear that what we'll get is a safe pair of hands from an obscure source with 'a problem with the vision thing'.

(Anon 1998: 3)

The shift in tone between the first part of this epistle and the last two sentences quoted is revealing. Does the potential difficulty in finding what the author claims to want in his or her institutional head have anything to do with the content and style of the musings that precede its expression?

This prompts some further thoughts about the role of humour within the higher education culture. It is clearly a key component in the everyday life of colleges and universities and is given extra spice by the role of such institutions as simultaneously both within and apart from (and hence able to be uniquely critical of) society as a whole. In the vast majority of cases its effect is liberating and its tone refreshing ('the principal is the shepherd of his flock, and the vice-principal is the crook on his staff'). However, as Rob Cuthbert and others have reminded us, it can also become vicious, and perhaps, as in the example quoted above, self-knowingly destructive of the enterprise as a whole (Cuthbert 1996: 197–202). 'Running' jokes can be particularly unhelpful in preserving and reinforcing stereotypes.

I have commented above (in the Introduction) about the myth and reality of 'new' management in colleges and universities. The bald fact remains that the UK system is almost invariably responsible for growing its own leadership; that is to say, heads of institutions and other senior managers rise through the ranks, however much they may feel (or be encouraged to feel) disengaged from their roots. Enthusiasm periodically surfaces, especially among 'independent' members of Boards of Governors for transfers in from the private sector, or even from other parts of the public sector, and it is true that there has been a smattering of former civil servants, captains of industry and management consultants among the ranks of the CVCP (Smith 1998). It is also true that in so far as such individuals have themselves been consumers (direct and indirect of the higher education product) their new working environment is more hospitable than would be, say, the Health Service to a non-career professional. But, in general, the academic community is responsible for its own.

Nor has the expansion of 'university' status changed this general truth. A recent study shows the advent of the '1992' institutions increasing the heterogeneity of the pool of institutional heads (and switching the modal discipline of their academic careers from science and humanities towards the social sciences), but only to a point. In 1997 the 'golden triangle' of Oxford, Cambridge and London still accounted for 47 per cent of vice-chancellors in post (Farnham and Jones 1998: 47).

Therein lie both strengths (loyalty, continuity, knowing the language and the terrain) and weaknesses (insularity, defensiveness, the 'not invented here' response to innovation). There is also the paradox, shared with schools, that as effective academics climb the management ladder, they leave behind more and more of the activity to which they owe their distinction: notably teaching and research. Nor does the material reward system necessarily help (crudely, and above a certain threshold, productive academics have always favoured time and professional support over simple cash in terms of remuneration). Vice-chancellors' salaries have broken away from the pack (in a pale imitation of those of the heads of the newly privatized industries), but institutions are often finding that the vital middle and senior positions (especially deanships and headship of departments) are insufficiently attractive for the cream of the professoriat; nor does the traditional approach of rotation of office at this level sit comfortably with the new pattern of internal and external demands.

For the strategic point of view this analysis heads in two directions: towards staff development for management and, more controversially, in favour of 'succession' planning.

As government and its agents (especially the TECs) have lined up to endorse the 'Investors in People' standard, the pressure has grown for HEIs to be more systematic, more comprehensive and more purposeful about their staff development strategies. For most categories of staff this implies being more analytical about the 'professional mix', for example of teaching, research and other activities (variously termed 'consultancy', 'technology transfer', 'knowledge exchange' or the more generous US formulation of 'service'). Buried in here is a special challenge for the development of leadership roles, on which the literature is extensive but largely unhelpful. As an area of study in higher education, it is perhaps disproportionately a victim of the 'soft ethnography' referred to in the Preface (Middlehurst 1993).

It is also prey to simple and reductionist hypothesis building. For example, an early report of a Leverhulme Trust-funded investigation into executive leadership in universities argues unequivocally that:

> changes in the relationship between state, society and its universities have reconfigured the nature of managerial leadership in contemporary higher education systems. Earlier charismatic

or collegial models of universal leadership have been replaced by a new model which emphasises managerial skills that are both bureaucratic and entrepreneurial.

(Smith *et al.* 1999: 284)

The authors concede that the UK system sits somewhat uncomfortably in the middle of a scale between least change in the USA (with its history of powerful executive presidents) and continental Europe (with its tradition of the elected rector). However, their own data on the UK case is very far from proving the simple existence of a 'new model', as they show vice-chancellors and principals struggling with the demands of strategic leadership, resource management and internal distribution in most cases as deeply conscious of the consensual nature of the academic community as they ever were.

The truth is, as usual, messier and more complex. What most honest accounts by academics thrust into senior management roles indicate is the necessity to get beyond 'common-sense' approaches to genuinely professional approaches to the trickier areas of institutional life at the turn of the century: on, for example, human resources, business planning, estates development, financial security and external relations. What the sensible chief executive (or aspirant chief executive) acknowledges, is that she or he will need help, from other senior professionals, and not just from the other side of an apartheid-style division of 'faculty' and 'administrative' roles.

Living with strategic management

Senior academic managers, especially in the UK, are wont to cry crocodile tears over their lot: unloved or even despised from inside and below; regarded as recidivist and ineffective from outside and above; buffeted by all of the storms raging around public services at the end of the twentieth century. They can often almost relish the impossibility of the task, as in Burton Clark's description of the 'demand overload' on universities – '[d]isjuncture is rooted in a simple fact: *demands on universities outrun their capacity to respond*' (Clark 1998: 128, original emphasis).

But they exaggerate. Academic leadership, and especially institutional headship, can be a source of pride and joy. Here is the former President of Cornell rallying the troops in the first number of a new publication of the American Council of Education, accurately, if grandly, entitled *The Presidency*:

The task of the college president, reduced to its essentials, is to define and articulate the mission of the institution; develop meaningful goals; and then recruit the talent, build the consensus, create the climate, and provide the resources to achieve them. All else is peripheral . . . And, if this task is demanding because the president is never 'off duty', it also is exhilarating and satisfying. The effective president will embody a level of energy and enterprise, of optimism and openness that is infectious. It is this spirit and the teamwork it promotes, that achieves success.

> (Rhodes 1998: 14–15; see also Aitkin 1998)

In conclusion, then, this essay has developed the character of a survival guide for the senior manager in carrying out his or her most sensitive task, as part-architect, part-steward of his or her institution's strategy. In this context a number of personal characteristics seem to be essential for survival and success. The most effective strategic leaders, first of all, retain respect for the core of their institutions' activities; they never forget who really does the work, whether it is research (for the RAE) or responsible assessment (for the maintenance of academic standards). Connected with this, they appear content with vicarious satisfaction and genuine pleasure in the achievements of others (staff and students). For example, the best leaders seed rather than announce their ideas (Ashby 1958: 72–3). Don Aitkin's antipodean perspective is typically forthright:

> leadership thus becomes a mixture of steering hard and cheering up. It is important . . . to believe in the direction, and (I say it without malice) somewhat unkind to the crew to set the course and then leave the boat suddenly to steer another one, perhaps larger or older.
>
> (Aitkin 1998: 124)

In practical terms, it is a cliché but true to identify communication as the most important skill. The best academic leaders I have observed have a kind of relentless good humour (at least at work) and never turn off the channels of communication. They also have to remember that courtesy is often a one-way street; they can be abused by members of the organization who genuinely believe that their own lack of manners is an indication of sincerity. Any lapse by way of a response in kind is, however, instantly a federal case. More positively they understand the symbolic significance of what they do and say. As Geoff Mulgan of Demos and the No 10 Policy Unit put it in an RSA symposium on 'leadership':

All leaders need to be able to construct narratives that make sense of the past and the future of their society or institution. To the extent that they are good story-tellers they draw more out of people, they add more meaning to their lives and that enables them to achieve things which would not otherwise be possible.

(RSA 1998: 77)

The modern social scientific term for this process is 'sense-making' (Taylor 1999: 139–40).

Pursuing the character analysis, the next quality has to be that of steadiness, and a commitment to helping people you work for and with to understand who you are and what you stand for. This is not incompatible with fallibility, and a preparedness to be wrong and act upon the discovery. Equally, it fits well with teamwork and the ability to delegate to and develop close colleagues.

The old-fashioned term for this combination of characteristics and abilities is 'good judgement'. For a long time it was assumed that judgement relied more on nature than nurture; that it could not be learned or developed. Such a view has undoubtedly contributed to the ethnic, gender, age and experiential homogeneity of the group running our colleges and universities. More recently, this truism has been challenged, in academia as well as industry. Good judgement, for example, comes very close to Daniel Goleman's concept of 'emotional intelligence', structured around the following five components:

- self-awareness (the ability to recognize and understand your moods, emotions and drives, as well as their effect on others);
- self-regulation (the ability to control or redirect disruptive impulses and moods; the propensity to suspend judgement – to think before acting);
- motivation (a passion to work for reasons that go beyond money or status; a propensity to pursue goals with energy and persistence);
- empathy (the ability to understand the emotional make-up of other people; skill in treating people according to their emotional reactions);
- social skill (proficiency in managing relationships and building networks; an ability to find common ground and build rapport) (Goleman 1998: 95).

Much as I have an aversion to management theory as popular psychology (especially when, as here, it is held to have a neuropharmacological basis), I do find this inventory of attributes empirically plausible. Institutional leaders who have succeeded in overcoming apparently intractable problems, do indeed appear to have characteristics like those above. Predictably, researchers at Henley Management College have begun to investigate the possibility of a systematic emotional quotient (EQ) test (Tysome 1999).

More importantly, Goleman asserts that emotional intelligence can be learned, despite its difficulty: for example, 'it is much harder to learn to emphasize – to internalize empathy as a natural response to people – than it is to become adept at regression analysis. But it can be done' (Goleman 1998: 97). The UK Industrial Society concurs. Through John Adair's 'Action-Centred Leadership' (ACL) approach they have concluded that 'leadership ability isn't an accident of birth, and that it can be defined by a set of skills, behaviours and actions which people can develop' (Lawson 1999: 11).

Finally, any prospective or actual strategic leader has to recognize that the exposure that goes with the top job is permanent and unrelenting. After all considerations, that is what your colleagues agree to pay you for.

The problem of power

Power relationships within universities are distinctly paradoxical. A very high profile individual leader, surrounded by a small functional team, heads an essentially flat organization, which tolerates hierarchy for limited practical reasons only, and cannot accept superior authority in the most important parts of its professional life. For much of industry 'flatness' is new and has led to unexpected tensions (Coulson-Thomas and Coe 1991: 21–2). In academia it has been a design principle since the beginning, as individuals and small teams have taken responsibility for both curriculum and academic standards. As the Dean of Westminster reminded the same RSA audience as Geoff Mulgan (pp. 95–6), 'institutions' are different from 'organizations'.

> An organisation exists to get something done and requires management while an institution is less concrete and is largely held together by people in the mind as part of their frame of reference. An institution is composed of the diverse fantasies and projections of those associated with it. These ideas are not consciously negotiated or agreed upon but they exist.
>
> (RSA 1998: 75)

This principle has had an unusual effect on power relations. Much ceremonial power is vested in the head of the institution, and many heads have been able to convert such power into broad and deep moral suasion. The best of them have also been able to walk the line between protection of their operation (by garnering resources, deflecting external attack, and acting as a lightning rod for unproductive controversy) and involvement (of all staff in understanding and 'owning' not only the institution's mission, but also a mature appreciation of its objective position). This latter point is particularly a case for mature judgement. Academics working at the cutting edge in both teaching and research will often prefer protection over involvement. This is one of the cases where knowledge does not necessarily set the agent free. A political–scientific approach to decision-making in academic communities defines the resulting balance as that between the use of traditional 'legitimation strategies' and 'pressure' (Bourgeois 1991: 23).

As Burton Clark puts the point, somewhat more brutally, 'universities are too bottom-heavy, too resistant from the bottom-up, for tycoons to dominate for very long' (Clark 1998: 4). There are analogues within faculties, departments and (to a lesser extent) support departments. But at the end of the day the reputation and standing of the institution rest with the lecturer marking examination papers, the Examination Board deciding degree classes, and the ethical commitments of the researcher. The resulting paradox is often not appreciated in the internal critique of hierarchy, which, as Richard Rorty has pointed out, can find hegemony everywhere – and nowhere (Rorty 1998: 94–6).

Appendix

THE UNIVERSITY CORPORATE PLAN: A WORKED EXAMPLE

This appendix offers, largely without commentary, some document-ary evidence of one institution (the author's own) remodelling its corporate and strategic plans at the end of the Millennium. The process began before, but concluded after, most of the external requirements and constraints listed in Chapters 2 and 3 were promulgated by the HEFCE and others.

The University of Brighton belongs to a group of former polytechnics incorporated by the 1988 Higher Education Act and granted both degree-awarding powers and its new title by the 1992 Further and Higher Education Act. Among this group – often misleadingly titled 'new' universities (its origins go back to the mid-nineteenth century) – it shares some characteristics with the majority (a strong professional and vocational emphasis, good civic links and a multi-site operation suffering from severe under-investment while under local authority control) but it is also in the minority of those with a strong balance sheet, significant successes in the two RAEs for which it has been eligible, and a well developed strategic planning partnership with its 'traditional' university neighbour. In 1999 it has over 16,000 students registered (nearly 6000 part-time, and approximately 1500 from outside the UK) in six faculties (Arts & Architecture, Business, Education & Sport, Health, Information Technology and Science & Engineering), across four main sites separated at the farthest point by 25 miles. The 1998–99 budget turnover is set at approximately £70 million.

A key internal communication device is the pair of publications *Channel* (largely news from and about the institution) and *Official Channel* (used for briefing and consultation on external and internal policy developments). Three of the four documents included below were distributed to all staff and governors of the institution as special numbers of *Official Channel*.

Between them they describe the most significant steps in the year-long process of recasting the university's Strategic Plan (subsequently renamed, in response to the HEFCE, the Corporate Plan). In approaching this material some health warnings are in order. These four chronological fence posts were joined by miles of consultative and deliberative wire, some of it as tangled as any you would find in an institutional culture like that of a university (see the Preface). In so far as the process was driven (or drivable) from the centre, it reflects the aspirations, commitments and, some would say the prejudices and blind spots of the author, as exposed in the previous three chapters.

Document 1 represents the baseline, the *Strategic Plan 1995–2000* as published by the university's Board of Governors and Academic Board on 1 April 1995.

Document 2 is the consultation paper *Reshaping the Strategic Plan, 1998–2003* published in January 1998.

Document 3 is a committee paper that went in almost identical form to the Academic Board and Board of Governors at the end of the 1997–98 academic session (paper B/33/98) reporting on the outcomes of consultation and revising the timetable.

Document 4 is the final version of the *Corporate Plan* as published in January 1999. A further internal publication, the *Strategic Plan* covering the same period, incorporates operational objectives and targets for their achievement. The university also produces (for its own purposes, as well as for submission to the Funding Council) an annual operating statement; this is in turn backed up by departmental, faculty and school operating statements showing responsibilities, targets and dates.

Document 1

Official Channel   Special Edition/April 1995
Strategic Plan 1995–2000

1 The planning context

The University of Brighton came into being on 1 September 1992, with degree-awarding powers under the 1992 Further and Higher Education Act. The new university builds upon a tradition of over 100 years of supplying high quality and accessible education in Brighton and Eastbourne.

This strategic plan supersedes that set by the former Brighton Polytechnic for the period 1992–96. During the previous planning period the institution achieved some significant successes: a decline in applications and market share from home and international students was arrested and turned into steady growth; external measures of quality were high; the employability record of graduates remained among the best in the country; research flourished and led to a strong performance in the first Research Assessment Exercise for which it was eligible; a number of estates projects was completed or begun (especially residences); and policies of benefit to the entire university were advanced (on staff development, equal opportunities, childcare and smoking). The result has been to confirm a role and reputation as one of the strongest of the new universities, building in particular upon the significant achievements of the polytechnic in bringing together academic and professional traditions in higher education.

The plan aims both to maintain this achievement and to assist the university in meeting new challenges and opportunities. These include the impact of the policies and funding mechanisms of the Higher Education Funding Council for England (HEFCE), the establishment of the Teacher Training Agency (TTA), the reversal of Government policy of expansion of student numbers, the prospect of new partnerships (for example with the National Health Service), new sources of support for research, and the continual requirement to match new social and economic needs for higher education. In this document the university's key aims and policies are summarised, together with the intended objectives and actions for the planning period. The university will continue to develop and approve annual operating statements setting out plans in more detail for each academic session.

2 Mission, aims and objectives

The corporate goal of the university is to be an institution of higher education accessible to all who can benefit and which emphasises excellence in teaching and learning, research, scholarship and creativity.

The university's underlying objectives are to:

- deliver both significant widening participation and high quality teaching and research within a single learning community;
- develop an academic profile carefully selected to combine achievement of its mission with the highest possible quality in those activities it chooses to undertake;
- extend the scope of joint planning for higher educational provision within the region through partnership with a broad range of institutions;
- continue to diversify its sources of income, support and collaboration.

The vision of the university which results is of an open, dynamic and responsive community of higher learning, with special strengths in professional and vocational applications, applied research and consultancy. It serves its students well in preparation for, and development within, employment, and its other clients in enhancing the economic, social and cultural life of the region. Its specific strengths are recognised nationally and internationally.

3 Academic profile

3.1 The academic programme

The university's academic programme consists of an overlapping and interconnected range of activities: full- and part-time undergraduate study; postgraduate and continuous professional development courses; services to commerce, industry and other public services; consultancy, and applied and basic research. Detailed academic planning will continue to recognise the mutually reinforcing nature of these activities.

The course portfolio of the university is soundly based and will continue to evolve. Some expansion will take place in subject areas in which the university is in a particularly strong position, both in its ability to attract applications and in its ability to offer high quality educational experience leading to strong employment prospects. This will entail consolidation in other areas. Indicative student numbers by mode and academic subject categories during the planning period are shown in Table 2.

The optimum size, physical location and departmental and faculty home of particular subject areas will be kept under regular review, recognising that the nature of academic development involves a process of growth, contraction and redrawing of boundaries within and between academic disciplines.

In addition to the need for academic development and renewal within existing disciplines, departments and faculties, the following university-wide developments will be achieved during the planning period:

- an integrated (applied and basic) science strategy for the university;
- a social sciences strategy;
- the clarification and further development of media studies.

The university will continue to seek to improve and expand its part-time provision, particularly by encouraging flexible patterns of delivery on both undergraduate and postgraduate courses and by planned support for continuous professional development (CPD) and continuing vocational education (CVE).

Building on the work of the Teaching and Learning Unit and through the processes of staff development, the university will continue to foster an educational environment where understanding of, and expertise in, methods of teaching and learning is regarded as indispensable for all those concerned with course delivery.

3.2 Research, consultancy and related activity

The university will continue to encourage and support the development and expansion of research, consultancy and related income generating activities. The expertise and facilities of the university as a whole will be made more accessible and responsive to the changing needs of the communities of which the university is a part.

All areas of academic work are planned to include a defined research programme. Decisions on developments in course offerings will continue to be taken in conjunction with those on research developments. The list of currently approved research programmes is included in Table 1.

Within all faculties and departments research activity and opportunities for research students will continue to expand on the basis of HEFCE funding and other funding opportunities. The rates of expansion will vary according to relative success in the Research Assessment Exercise, the university's decisions regarding selective investment, and the degree of success in securing external funding.

Efforts will concentrate on building on existing relationships by expansion and promotion of supporting consultancy, applied testing, training and advisory services as part of the university's 'Services to Business' initiative as coordinated by the Joint Marketing Unit. Special emphasis will be placed upon development of research, consultancy and related training activities to meet the business and technological needs of small and medium-sized enterprises (SMEs) within the region. Further steps will be taken to support the exploitation of innovation and intellectual property.

The research policy and aims of the university are thus to foster individual and joint initiatives within an agreed framework of broad goals and common processes of research management.

4 Partnerships

4.1 Regional collaboration

The university will continue to play an active and constructive role within the local and regional community. Key focuses for this activity include the Sussex Academic Corridor project and the university's Teaching Company

Centre. Relationships with partner colleges and with local schools, industry, commerce and other public services will remain high priorities for attention. A clear strategy for seeking, agreeing to or refusing active educational and commercial partnerships will be developed.

4.2 International collaboration

The university reaffirms its commitment to Europe and projects involving European partners. Greater coordination will be achieved by the establishment of the university's European Office and steps taken to:

- develop a European orientation within selected taught courses;
- recruit students from across the European Union (EU);
- mount courses leading to joint awards with strategically selected European institutions;
- seek EU research or development funded projects;
- develop links with non-EU countries.

Approved links with other international partners will continue to be developed, including through the American Office and with Japan, Brazil and Malaysia.

Attention will also be paid to improving the recruitment and continued support of international students and strengthening relationships with overseas alumni organizations.

5 Academic organisation and priorities

The university remains committed to organising its academic work through a small number of faculties, whose composition and structure are kept under regular review. Through the committee structure of the Academic Board and faculty boards it aims to ensure that there are opportunities for all staff to play a part in the shaping of their subjects and the university's academic programme. The academic community accepts its responsibility to ensure that new developments, growth, contraction and interlinking of areas of academic work can be effectively managed and delivered.

Forms of academic organisation, learning support and resource allocation will be maintained that contribute to the increase in opportunities for inter-faculty courses, to the university-wide development and sharing of good practice in teaching and learning, and to collaboration in research, consultancy and delivery of services to the community.

To support the work of faculties and to encourage collaboration between faculties and between the university and other institutions, a number of university-wide developments will be pursued:

- the further development of university undergraduate and postgraduate modular frameworks;

- the creation of more effective means of developing and sharing good practice in teaching and learning;
- the progressive rationalisation of the academic year for standard courses around a 30-week two-semester model;
- provision of personal support services for students which will more effectively combine the expertise and resources of teaching and central departments;
- a learning environment which supports independent learning through the provision of a wide range of information in a variety of media, and through the use of appropriate technology to deliver programmes on and beyond the campuses.

The university will ensure that its formal approaches to standards and quality relate not only to academic standards and the quality of teaching and research, but also to the many other dimensions of the institution's life, including the quality of working life it offers to its members and the services it offers to its clients. A university charter will be developed, and use will be made of national and international standards and initiatives when these are deemed to be of value.

The university will continue to engage constructively with national systems of peer review and academic regulation, and further develop its own systems for establishing and maintaining academic health.

6   Staff and staff development

Staff development is an integral part of the working life of each member of staff, and is associated with both an individual's own developmental needs and the requirements of the university's strategic development. The university will continue to develop an understanding and delivery of staff development which involves all staff equally as partners in achieving the aims of the university.

Neither the maintenance of current successful performance nor the achievement of significant change will be possible without staff who are both committed to the university's objectives and in possession of the necessary skills to achieve them. To ensure this the university will strengthen the current staff development policy to ensure its implementation in all departments and its relevance for all members of staff. Other commitments include:

- the further development and support of flexibility of duties for individual staff;
- the avoidance of compulsory redundancy as a means of effecting change in staffing patterns; a model will be agreed for understanding, planning for, and accepting growth and contraction in staff numbers within different departments of the university to meet identified needs;
- the establishment of explicit professional models for teaching and research staff;

- the establishment of 'management development' as an appropriate professional model for senior administrative and all managerial staff;
- reaffirmation of the goal of equality of opportunity including the setting of interim targets and annual plans of action under the equal opportunities policy.

7   The working environment

7.1   Central support services

The services provided by central departments play an important part both in the achievement of high quality teaching and research and also in the creation of the environment within which our staff and students work and study. A systematic review will be undertaken to establish the appropriate size, location and responsibilities of central services in order to underpin the strategic objectives of the university. In particular central services will be developed to support effective course delivery and research activity as well as to facilitate inter-faculty cooperation and that with external partners.

Attention will be paid in the period to 2000 to the quality of the whole student experience, including the creation of an information-rich environment increasingly accessed through strategies of independent learning, of a comfortable and secure physical environment for study and residence, and of cultural, leisure and sporting facilities.

Customer service standards will be developed for central services, so that these can be scrutinised by staff, students and external clients.

The effective management of existing activities and the development of realistic and effective future plans depends critically upon the availability of accurate and high quality information. The university plans to review and improve its information systems, drawing upon best practice within and beyond the higher education sector.

The Brighton Graduates Association will be developed and steps taken to expand the university community to include its considerable number of former students in the UK and overseas.

7.2   The university estate

The university's estates strategy has been published in conjunction with this strategic plan and lodged with the funding council. Further development will be informed and shaped by the needs of adjusted faculty and departmental boundaries.

Specific projects to be addressed during the planning period include the completion of the new Moulsecoomb library, rationalisation and improvement of library and academic space at Eastbourne, the first stage of the redevelopment of Grand Parade and new residential accommodation within the town of Brighton and at Falmer.

During the planning period the university will continue its programme of building maintenance and refurbishment, informed by an environmental strategy designed to assist the continuous improvement of the physical working environment for all members of the university. A high priority within this strategy will be the improvement of security, where the university aims to minimise risks to people and property while maintaining an open and accessible institution.

8 Financial resource and planning

Financial policy will continue to be based around prudent financial planning to ensure that sufficient provision is made for known and unanticipated liabilities, so that these will not deflect the university from the achievement of its primary objectives. In addition, we will creatively consider all development opportunities that will improve quality or increase net income.

The university faces a period of reduced real terms recurring funding from the funding council at a time when we need to pursue an energetic programme of refurbishment, redevelopment and replacement of buildings, plant and equipment, to maintain staff security and to continue to improve the quality of our mainstream teaching and research activity. The university will therefore seek to develop further its strategy for diversification of income away from over dependence on any single funding source. As part of this strategy, business plans for the university's trading and services companies will be actively pursued.

The university has been well served by its policy of devolved budget management and this will continue within the agreed framework of financial regulations and procedures. Particular difficulties arise in relation to the timely replacement of equipment relating to teaching and research. We shall seek to maximise resources available for this purpose from both corporate and local funding sources.

The university has undertaken a number of long-term borrowing commitments in relation to new accommodation. At the same time a cash management policy seeks to maximise funds available for investment. We will publish and monitor performance against a Treasury management policy that ensures that best, but prudent, use is made of internal cash resources in order to minimise the costs of borrowing.

Indicative financial forecasts for the planning period are shown in Figure 1.

The financial forecast takes as its starting point projected student numbers. An assessment is made of likely income from the HEFCE and Teacher Training Agency (TTA) grant, from LEA and other tuition fees and from other income sources. These assessments take account of announcements made by the Government and the funding bodies as to the rates at which income will be increased for inflation and also the reductions or efficiency gains that will be made. The assessment also takes account of local targets to increase income from research, consultancy and continuing professional development courses.

The assessment of expenditure takes account of the policy of the Board of Governors to maintain uncommitted revenue reserves at £2 million after 1995/96, the requirement of the HEFCE to fund fully our long-term maintenance plan, and planned additional commitments such as the new library at Moulsecoomb.

During the planning period the trust responsible for the university's Foundation Fund will be established to oversee specific projects in support of the university's activities.

9 The university community

A vital element in the university's achievement of its goal and objectives is the cohesiveness and common purpose of the community. The university places a high priority on student and staff involvement in decision making, and on open governance. At the same time it recognises the disciplines involved in living and working within a purposive community and the need for the utmost integrity and accountability on the part of those chosen to manage its affairs.

The shared values reaffirmed by the staff, students and governors of the university of Brighton are republished with this plan as a framework of aspiration and intention for our collective endeavours.

- We do not discriminate unfairly either directly or indirectly against members or prospective members of our community.
- We acknowledge and value our corporate independence and accept the responsibilities and rights it embodies.
- We value academic freedom of thought and its appropriate expression without let or hindrance.
- We value the participation of members of the university community in its corporate activities and its decision-making processes.
- We accept and value our responsibilities to facilitate the personal and professional development of all members of the community.

Approved by the Academic Board
Approved by the Board of Governors
April 1995

Document 1, Table 1   Approved research programmes 1995

Art, Design and Humanities	• Design History Research Centre • Rediffusion Simulation Research Centre NB: Research activity within the faculty also comprises scholarly enquiry in history, philosophy, history of art, cultural studies and critical theory – and creative work, through exhibitions, publication, composition and performance, in painting, printmaking, film, dance, music, graphic design, illustration, photography and design.

Document 1, Table 1 (*cont'd*)

Business School	• Centre for Research in Innovation Management • Capital Markets Research Unit • Financial Decisions Research Group • International Business Unit • Linguistics Research Unit • Manager Learning Research Unit • Media Technology in Languages Unit • Tourism Research Unit
Education, Sport and Leisure	• Chelsea School Research Centre • Teaching and Learning Research Centre NB: The Chelsea School Research Centre comprises two research clusters: Adherence, Performance and Attrition; and Sport and Leisure. The Teaching and Learning Research Centre is currently being restructured to reflect areas of work in literacies, exclusion and diversity, higher education policy and management, and teaching and learning.
Engineering and Environmental Studies	• Applied Image Processing Research Unit • Architecture and Building Research Unit • Control and Dynamics Research Unit • Earth and Environmental Science Research Unit • Heat Transfer Research Unit • Hydraulic Engineering Research Unit • Power Electronics and Energy Research Unit • Power Engineering Research Unit • Structural Timber Research Unit
Health	• Clinical Research Unit • Health and Social Policy Research Centre • Nursing Research Unit • Pharmaceutical Sciences Research Group
Information Technology	• Information Technology Research Institute • Social and Educational Application of knowledge Engineering NB: Research within the Departments of Computing, Mathematical Sciences and Library and Information Studies is predominantly organized through more informal groupings within the departments and faculty. Current major areas include software engineering, formal methods, finite elements, information industry innovation and multimedia.

Document 1, Table 2 Student number plans 1994/95 to 1998/99

Full-time (taught programmes and research)	1994/5		1995/6		1996/7		1997/8		1998/9	
	HEFCE funded	Other	HEFCE funded	Other	HEFCE funded	Other	HEFCE funded	Other	HEFCE funded	Other
Subjects allied to medicine	199	1700	220	1600	220	1600	220	1600	220	1600
Science	1022	68	970	70	950	70	950	70	950	70
Engineering	783	113	750	115	725	120	725	120	725	120
Built environment	512	17	515	20	500	20	500	20	500	20
Maths, IT and computing	1007	35	980	40	950	45	950	50	950	55
Business and management	1618	67	1620	70	1620	75	1620	80	1620	80
Social sciences	254	2	275	5	295	10	290	10	290	10
Humanities	405	1	450	5	470	5	470	5	470	5
Art and design	910	34	950	38	1000	40	1050	40	1090	40
Initial teacher education	1210	11	0	1220	0	1210	0	1210	0	1210
Education	29	8	25	8	25	8	25	8	25	8
Total	7949	2056	6755	3191	6755	3203	6800	3213	6840	3218

Part-time (taught programmes and research)	1994/5		1995/6		1996/7		1997/8		1998/9	
	HEFCE funded	Other	HEFCE funded	Other	HEFCE funded	Other	HEFCE funded	Other	HEFCE funded	Other
Subjects allied to medicine	293	30	331	30	340	30	340	30	340	30
Science	172	21	156	24	175	24	175	24	175	24
Engineering	166	0	154	0	175	0	175	0	175	0
Built environment	146	0	165	0	170	0	170	0	170	0
Maths, IT and computing	123	0	155	0	185	0	209	0	215	0
Business and management	917	0	1067	0	1100	0	1100	0	1100	0
Social sciences	76	0	87	0	85	0	85	0	85	0
Humanities	191	0	255	0	300	0	300	0	300	0
Art and design	51	0	105	0	238	0	250	0	250	0
Initial teacher education	13	0	0	0	0	0	0	0	0	0
Education	706	0	700	0	700	0	700	0	700	0
Total	2854	51	3175	54	3468	54	3504	54	3510	54

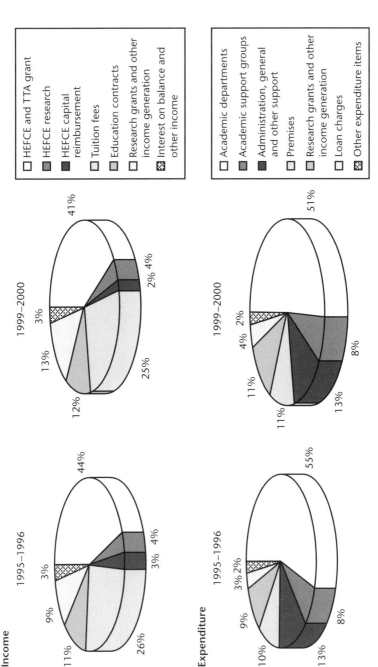

Document 1, Figure 1 Financial forecasts 1995–2000: Total income and expenditure is anticipated to grow from £63m in 1995–96 to £69m in 1999–2000

Document 2 ■

Official Channel   **Special Edition January 1998**
Reshaping the Strategic Plan 1998–2003

The university's current strategic plan, for the period 1995–2000, was approved by Academic Board and Board of Governors on 1 April 1995. It was designed to be a realistic set of goals enabling us to plan through to the end of the century. In fact, although it proved appropriate to the challenges facing the university during the first two years of the period, the environment in which the higher education sector as a whole operates is set to change as a result of a number of external influences. For this reason, the two Boards have decided that this is the right time to reshape the strategic plan and to consider revised goals and targets.

The Strategic Plan 1998–2003 will be developed over the next six months, through a process of consultation inside the university and with outside organisations with which we work closely. In this special edition of *Official Channel*, we begin that process by outlining the results of initial discussions on the new plan by the Director's Management Group. These follow initial consultations including a joint seminar between the Academic Board and Board of Governors in October 1997. Inside, we review the university's achievements against the objectives in the Strategic Plan 1995–2000 and outline the main aspects of the external environment that we must bear in mind as we develop the new plan. A loose-leaf insert explains how the consultation process will work and how you can become involved in it.

Towards the Strategic Plan 1998–2003

In 1995 the vision of the university was of:

> An open, dynamic and responsive community of higher education with special strengths in professional and vocational applications, applied research and consultancy. It serves its students well in preparation for, and development within, employment, and its other clients in enhancing the economic, social and cultural life of the region. Its specific strengths are recognised nationally and internationally.

Much of this is still relevant today. If we have changed our corporate view since the last plan was produced, it is to emphasise the continuum between vocational and non-vocational higher education. In the university's response to the National Committee of Inquiry into Higher Education (NCIHE) – the most recent statement giving a sense of our collective vision – we indicated that we see both vocational and non-vocational higher education coexisting in a broader framework:

> There is . . . a broad continuum between courses whose aims include a particular professional qualification, followed typically by a very specific

career path . . . and those which do not. It is a fundamental principle for universities, such as Brighton, which define professional and vocational education as central to their mission, that higher education designed for vocational purposes should foster intellectual development, personal maturity and transferable skills no less than other courses of equivalent standard. Professional and vocational education should . . . prepare our future specialist professional engineers, business managers, designers, information technologists, health professionals and teachers to gain the skills, the knowledge, the intellectual vision, the creativity and the ambition to go beyond our current definitions and understandings, to reform, revitalise and transform their professions – to be the leaders in that process . . .

We support the view that there is no need to abandon the main principles and objectives set out in the Robbins Report concerning the personal, social, economic and global aims and purposes of higher education.

We see 'education for social and economic purpose' as the vision for the University of Brighton in 1998–2003.

The key messages

The external factors outlined inside are pointers to the kind of strategy which we will need to develop. The following is not a comprehensive list. However, it sets the scene for reflection on the strategic priorities, detailed in the final section. We will need:

- all members of the university to be knowledgeable about the university's overall academic strategy, to be comfortable with a shared vision of the future, and to be confident about communicating that vision;
- to develop a distinctive mission for the University of Brighton which selects from, and maintains the best of, the values of our history while rising to new challenges;
- to manage the balance between, on one hand, flexibility of response to changed external factors and circumstances and, on the other, guaranteed and assured quality of teaching, research and related activity;
- to improve continuously the physical and working environment in which members of the university community study, work and live;
- to collaborate constructively with regional partners in the interests of regional economic and social development.

Features of the Strategic Plan 1995–2000

The Strategic Plan 1995–2000 took a cautious approach to the future and therefore proved to be appropriate for the environment of 1995–97. Many of the major strategic objectives which we set for 1995–2000 are still fully to be achieved. Nevertheless we achieved interim goals against all of the key objectives.

A detailed analysis of progress against objectives is given in the annual reviews of the University's 'operating statements' (presented to the Academic Board each June). Here we summarise achievements in key areas, with examples of our achievements shown under each of the key objectives in the Strategic Plan 1995–2000. These provide a platform for the development of continuing and new objectives for 1998–2003. Prudent financial management has also meant that we enter this new planning period with forecast break-even revenue budgets and modest reserves, enabling an effective response to unforeseen events and continuation of estates projects in particular.

Progress against our strategic objectives

- **To keep under regular review the optimum size, physical location and departmental and faculty home of particular subject areas.**
  The re-organisation of the university to be implemented in 1998/9 has been agreed and the associated administrative review is currently being carried out.
- **To seek to improve and expand the university's part-time provision**
  Part-time student numbers have grown by 28 per cent during the first two years of the planning cycle.
  We have been awarded funding for special initiatives to develop continuing vocational education and continuing education provision.
- **To encourage and support the development and expansion of research, consultancy and related income generating activity**
  Members of the university improved their scores in 11 of the 20 units submitted in the Research Assessment Exercise undertaken by the funding council.
  Competitive research grant successes have been achieved in key areas such as CENTRIM, Information Technology Research Institute (ITRI), Pharmacy, Civil Engineering and the Design History Research Centre.
  Consultancy has continued to expand, and substantial industrial sponsorships have been obtained.
  We have developed a code of practice for intellectual property rights.
  The Teaching Company Scheme has continued to expand.
- **To continue to play an active and constructive role within the local and regional community, to put in place university-wide developments in support of the work of faculties, and to encourage collaboration between faculties and between the university and other institutions.**
  Links with key local and regional players have continued to be fostered, including the University of Sussex, East and West Sussex County Councils, Brighton and Hove Council, Sussex Enterprise, and further education and sixth form colleges; partnership funding has been received from the Single Regeneration Budget as well as the Government Office for the South-East (GOSE).

Electronic networking of the various university campuses has been completed.

- **To continue to improve overall standards and methods of teaching and learning, and to develop further our systems for establishing and maintaining quality which relate to academic standards, teaching and research, environment and support.**

  The latest round of funding council teaching quality assessment visits has resulted in Languages, the History of Art, Architecture and Design, and Civil Engineering all achieving highly commendable results.

  In the recent OFSTED inspections of PGCE secondary courses in Business Education and Religious Education, all categories were rated as either very good or good.

  A policy for accreditation of all teaching staff has been agreed.

- **To continue to develop an understanding and delivery of staff development which involves all staff equally as partners**

  We have appointed a staff development manager and have confirmed the policy on staff development.

  A job-sharing scheme has been established.

- **To pay attention to the quality of the whole student experience**

  A project to ascertain the needs of part-time students is in progress with a view to improving access to facilities for these students.

  We have agreed university standards on personal tutoring and on careers education.

  The Workshop has been established to help students find part-time work.

  University graduates and diplomates continue to perform strongly in the job market.

- **To execute the estates strategy, and to continue the programme of building maintenance and refurbishment**

  Marked progress has been made towards improving the physical environment for the whole university community.

  Significant developments have taken place within the university estate: the Aldrich Library at Moulsecoomb; improved and new student residences at Varley, Falmer and the Phoenix sites; a bus route for the Falmer campus; the first phase of the fourth wing at Grand Parade.

- **To develop further the university's strategy for diversification of income and maximisation of funding council income**

  The total number of international (i.e. non-UK) students in the university has risen year on year to its highest ever point of over 1,500.

  Three development schemes with the private sector have been undertaken which could not have been achieved solely from university resources: Blackwell's bookshop and cafe in Cockcroft; student residences at Falmer; Brighton Health and Racquet Club at Falmer, which has raised significant funds for future investment for the benefit of the university community.

The changing environment

Almost immediately following the publication of our last Strategic Plan, the environment in which the university was operating changed substantially. The prospects for mainstream public funding deteriorated dramatically. The previous period of growth in the number of students in higher education, particularly full-time undergraduates, was reversed. The government also significantly reduced earmarked public funding for capital expenditure. Responsibility for student number allocations and funding of teacher training moved to the Teacher Training Agency (TTA).

The university entered its last planning period in the context of a reduction in unit funding across the sector which precipitated the funding crisis in part leading to the setting up of the NCIHE. Perhaps the single most important influence on the university community as we plan for the new millennium is the report of the NCIHE published in July 1997. It is regarded as the most important and wide-ranging report on higher education since the Robbins Report in 1963. The government's response (and to other reports such as the Kennedy report, *Learning Works*, and that of the National Advisory Group for Continuing Education and Lifelong Learning) is expected in a white paper on Lifelong Learning due early in 1998 and will have far reaching effects. It is important that we are well positioned to deal with the recommendations and their implications.

As we embark upon the current planning process, the main external influences are as follows.

The report of the NCIHE

The key messages in the Dearing report are:

- the need for an expansion of higher education of 50 per cent, mainly at sub-degree level
- the need for tougher measures to safeguard standards
- enhanced professionalism in teaching
- new funding for research
- greater use of ICTs
- a warning against reducing short-term funding
- graduate contributions towards the cost of tuition
- a stronger regional and community role for higher education
- a review of pay and working practices.

The impact of New Labour

The government's approach to the proposals on full-time undergraduate tuition fees in the Dearing report is well known. Also important are policy changes in relation to part-time students: for example, their eligibility for Access Funds.

The government's reaction to the other proposals in the Dearing, Kennedy and Fryer reports is awaited in the White Paper and associated policy statements, but there are already signs of its emerging strategy. Increasing participation is top of the agenda. Under-represented groups, particularly the lower socio-economic classes and disaffected young adults, are going to be targeted. Plans have been announced to fund 500,000 extra places in further and higher education by 2002 – with probably up to 80 per cent of these in the further education sector. Other key government initiatives include the 'University for Industry' and Regional Development Agencies.

Funding for higher education will be relatively stable in 1998/9 with any additional funds only serving to reduce the level of the cut. There is still significant uncertainty about 1999/2000 and beyond.

The Quality Assurance Agency

Quality and standards are likely to be high on the agenda. Changes will take place to the subject review process, formerly known as teaching quality assessment, and potentially in other areas such as external examining, audit of overseas and collaborative provision, and institutional review. While our core systems and processes are currently very sound, they will necessarily have to evolve.

Changes to funding

The methodology for calculating the grant income which we receive from the Higher Education Funding Council for England (HEFCE) is being simplified. From 1998/9 our contract will consist of a single number of full-time equivalents (FTEs) funded according to three different price groups.

By contrast, the TTA contract for initial teacher training will be disaggregated into sub-targets which must be individually met. The future funding of our largely part-time continuing professional development (CPD) in teacher training (INSET) will be subject to a system of competitive bidding. This will mean a greater degree of external control and influence.

Funding for courses in professions allied to medicine will transfer from the HEFCE to the Department of Health from 1998/9. The evolving training and R&D strategies of the NHS will require careful analysis, and continued success in this area will increasingly depend upon establishing and maintaining sound strategic alliances with the NHS and its agencies.

There will be changes too in the way the university receives fee income with the introduction of means tested tuition fees for full-time undergraduate students from 1998/9.

The European and international context

Changes within the European Union of relevance to our future plans are:

- opportunities for funding, for example of regional projects;
- 'enlargement' and the prospect of further collaboration in central and eastern Europe;

- the impact of the EMU;
- the Fifth Framework for research programmes, which will commence in 1998/9.

We already have good structures in place to turn these changes into opportunities for the university. It will be important to balance the costs against the benefits. The Fifth Framework deserves particular mention because of the close fit between its thematic areas and our own research interests: life sciences and technologies; information and communication technologies; transport, mobility and production; energy, environment and sustainable development. In addition generic research areas prioritised for funding include innovation and the participation of SMEs, and improving human potential by the training of research personnel.

The changing nature of global and local economies causes the wider international market to be more volatile and less predictable. Institutionally we are not as advanced in the international arena as we are in Europe. However, with the establishment of the International Relations Office, a strategy is in place to establish a structure for international developments and recruitment. Partnerships are likely to be selective and deliberately diverse to match the different interests of the countries and regions with which we might establish links. Focal areas are likely to be Malaysia, Hong Kong and China, Japan, India, South Africa, parts of South America and Taiwan.

Characteristics of the Sussex region

The Sussex region remains strategically important for the university. However, there are mixed characteristics of the university's locality.

In Brighton there are stark contrasts. A lower percentage of school students achieve five or more GCSEs at grades A* to C than the national average. By contrast the percentage of graduates in the workforce in Brighton is higher than the national average. The picture in Sussex as a whole is quite different with a higher than average achievement at GCSE but a lower graduate workforce.

In Sussex average hourly earnings are below the UK average and there is a much higher proportion of small and medium-sized enterprises (SMEs).

The established key local industries are financial services, tourism, retail, and education both Government funded and commercial. Emerging industries include multi-media and advanced engineering. Key issues for the economic strategy include: links between the universities and industry; strengthening support for SMEs and strengthening key industries with growth potential.

Partnerships

Probably the greatest threat to all education institutions in the late 1990s is failure to collaborate and to form constructive regional partnerships. We have already made significant progress in developing partnerships of all kinds.

From this base we will develop mature working relationships with existing partners and explore arrangements with new partners.

Commitment to partnerships is evident from our wish to share our high level objectives with partners at the earliest stage in the planning process, and to use the outcome of consultation with partners to inform the development of our new strategic plan.

Existing key partnerships which we will enhance are with:

- the University of Sussex
- schools, sixth form colleges and general FE colleges in the region
- Health Authorities, Trusts and NHS regional consortia
- Brighton & Hove Council and East and West Sussex County Councils
- Sussex Enterprise
- the South of England Accreditation Network (SEANET)
- the Government Office for the South-East
- local and regional companies especially SMEs
- Taylor's College in Malaysia.

Those partnerships to foster include

- with the new Regional Development Agency
- research links with other universities, for example, the Universities of Portsmouth, Southampton and Surrey
- the new National Sports Academy.

There is potential for the university to work with our partners to make a positive impact on economic development of the region; for example, with East Sussex County Council in Eastbourne and Hastings. With corporate partners we should aim to develop a holistic approach, covering staff development, research and consultancies; these will be facilitated by members of the newly formed Business Services Office working closely with those in faculties and schools.

The Academic Corridor project was set up in 1993 as a collaborative venture between the Universities of Brighton and Sussex and Brighton College of Technology to promote the expertise, facilities and services of the three institutions to business, industry and the local community. With the re-launch of the project early in 1998, there is the prospect of further capitalising on this venture and of expanding it to include other partners.

Strategic priorities

Under various headings below are high level generic strategic priorities, which have emerged from the discussion so far on the shape of the new strategic plan. These will be further developed into strategic goals as a result of responses to this paper from the whole university community, from the Board of Governors, Academic Board and their committees, as well as from external partners. The resulting strategic plan for the period 1998–2003 will be published in August 1998.

Academic structures and portfolio

- to enhance our academic portfolio so that more of what we offer is at the same standard and quality as its current best elements
- to adjust the academic portfolio to ensure that it meets the needs of current and potential students, by revising courses and agreeing plans for growth and contraction
- to plan for the expected demand for more part-time and mixed-mode study
- to simplify, where possible, academic frameworks, academic regulations and awards titles so that greater effort can be focused on core academic activity, and less on academic administration
- to sustain high-quality teaching and seek further developments and improvements where necessary, with the aim of enabling us to cooperate efficiently and effectively in quality assurance processes
- to develop the research strategy in such a way that it will deliver significant improvements in the next Research Assessment Exercise, to extend the range and quality of commercially and Research Council funded research, and to support the scholarly activity of all teaching staff
- to capitalise on the significant work already undertaken to network the sites of the university and to make greater use of information and communications technologies (ICTs).

Support for members of the university community

- to support members of the university community by being careful of their working conditions and the quality of their working lives
- to identify the further needs of the university's communities for continuing professional development, including accreditation of teaching staff, and to ensure that provision is in place to meet those needs
- to consider all aspects of students' experience including student services, guidance and support, studying and living arrangements, and part-time employment
- to progress further the already established policies on equal opportunities including response to the Disability Discrimination Act

Partnerships and community role

- to collaborate with local authorities on their strategies for the social and economic development of our geographical region with particular emphasis on Eastbourne, Hastings, Brighton & Hove, and Worthing
- to extend existing, and to form new, collaborative partnerships with Further Education Funding Council-funded colleges in the region to provide opportunities for curriculum and staff development for widening participation; and in particular to support associate colleges in developing further and expanding their HE provision at certificate diploma level

- to develop further the already strong relationship with the National Health Service for the provision of a wide range of educational and training services; also to support the NHS research and development strategy by working with local trust
- to develop selective international and European links in support of our academic strategy

Environment and support services

- to continue the development of the Estate Strategy to benefit the university's community and to enable us to achieve our academic plans
- to improve further facilities across the university with a particular focus on the Falmer and Eastbourne campuses
- to establish systems and procedures to enable members of the university to monitor performance, to maximise its position in respect of funding arrangements and to provide a high quality service to its community.

'Insert' Reshaping the Strategic Plan 1998–2003
– the consultation process

All members of the university community are invited to take part in the consultation process to reshape the University of Brighton's Strategic Plan 1998–2003. Comments are welcome on the external environment, and the vision and strategic priorities outlined in sections 2 and 3 of this special edition of *Official Channel*. Some specific questions to stimulate discussion are given below. However, you need not confine your discussion to these questions.

Your comments will be used to inform the production of the version of the Strategic Plan to be put to Academic Board and Board of Governors for final approval in the summer of 1998, and to be published in August 1998. The plan will contain specific goals to be drawn from agreed priorities established via the consultation. A sensitivity analysis will also be undertaken to consider the effects of not being able to accomplish various aspects of the plan over the five year period.

In this phase of consultation we are focusing on high-level plans only. Faculties and schools, departments and units will have the opportunity to contribute to the setting of strategic goals and operational targets at a later stage. Once the Strategic Plan 1998–2003 has been agreed, faculties will find it helpful to develop complementary plans to sit alongside and feed into the overall university plan. These will be used to set year-on-year institutional targets.

Consultation within the university community will be via the Committee structure during the spring term, and also by more informal means through all faculties, schools, departments and units. Feedback from these meetings will be via your dean, head of school, department or unit at a meeting of directorate, deans and heads of department at the end of this term. There will also be a series of open meetings on each site to hear your comments. Times dates and places are:

5 March, 4.30–6pm, Sallis Benney Theatre, Grand Parade
6 March, 1–2.30pm, Greynore Hall, Eastbourne
13 March, 1–2.30pm, Mithras House, G8 Moulsecoomb
16 March, 4.30–6pm, Asa Briggs, Falmer

The consultation process will involve not only members of the university community but also key external partners. This will ensure that our partners are involved in the construction of the high-level objectives underlying our Strategic Plan. The aim is to create a forum for debate ensuring that the key collaborative partnerships in Sussex provide the same sense of overall direction for the regional community.

Key strategic questions

On the vision and priorities underlying the Strategic Plan 1998–2003

Do you endorse the main goal of the university as 'education for social and economic purpose'?

What are the most important characteristics of the University of Brighton to retain and develop?

Have any high-level strategic priorities been missed on the back page?

How should we respond to the Government policy on lifelong learning?

What criteria should we use to decide whether or not to introduce a new subject into our portfolio or to develop a particular award bearing course?

Is it essential to have significant research activity in all subject areas represented in the university's portfolio?

What criteria should we use to decide where we develop international links?

Do you re-affirm the shared values as stated in the Strategic Plan 1995–2000?

On the changing environment

What significant characteristics of the Sussex region have been missed?

What local and regional organisations should we link with, for what purpose and how should links be created?

Do you agree that the key messages on the front page capture what our underlying strategy should be?

Document 3

THE UNIVERSITY OF BRIGHTON   B/33/98
BOARD OF GOVERNORS

Strategic Plan: report on progress

1   Consultation process

1.1   Within the University community

1.1.1   The insert in the special edition of *Official Channel* on reshaping the Strategic Plan published in January 1998 detailed the process of consultation, both formal and informal, within the University community:

- via the committee structure in the Spring Term;
- informal meetings in faculties, schools, departments and units with feedback via the Deans and Heads;
- open meetings on each site in March.

1.1.2   The vision of the future direction of the faculties, schools, departments and units was also considered at the senior staff seminars on strategic planning held just before Easter.

1.2   With key external players

1.2.1   Groups of key external players with whom to consult on the production of the Strategic Plan were identified by the University's Management Group. Different letters were sent out under the Director's signature to each group. The letters invited general comments from all groups, if they felt inclined, and responses to particular questions from the group including our local and regional educational partners, and local and regional councils. Consultation with partner primary and secondary schools took place via the Partnership in Education Committees in the Faculty of Education, Sport and Leisure.

1.2.2   Details of the groups and the responses are given below.

	Group	Number in group	Number of responses
(i)	VIPs including local MPs, MEPs, mayors	22	9
(ii)	Honorary graduates and fellows	38	8
(iii)	Professional and Statutory Bodies which accredit our courses TTA, HEFCE, CVCP International partners	33	5
(iv)	GOSE, Sussex Enterprise, Chief Executives of County Councils and	11	6

	Brighton & Hove Council, Leaders of District Councils		
(v)	Members of business community	37	6
(vi)	Local FEFC funded colleges, universities of Sussex, Surrey, Portsmouth, Chichester Institute, Chief Executive of regional LEAs, regional Health Trusts	34	8
(vii)	Community groups	3	0

1.2.3   Although the overall response rate at 23% was somewhat disappointing, the external consultation is considered to have been a worthwhile exercise since respondees appeared to welcome the opportunity to be involved. There was considerable support for the approach to regional collaboration and forming constructive partnerships. Perhaps most disappointing was the level of response from educational partners although this group showed an interest in meeting to discuss further shared plans.

2   Key points arising from the internal consultation

2.1   Open meetings and committees

2.1.1   Feedback on the University's mission and vision statement suggests that it is somewhat limited. There was an absence of the benefits of 'learning for its own sake'. The statement needed to extend beyond the merely instrumental. It was felt that it lacked cultural, creative and educative aspects. Suggestions for additions included 'learning', 'cultural', 'environmental', 'vocational', 'professional'.

2.1.2   It was generally believed that the University existed to improve and assist society and individuals within it, to help them to lead better, richer and fuller lives both personal and professional. Therefore the emphasis on partnerships in *Official Channel* was too much at the corporate level and should also include individuals and community groups. The University's approach to 'widening access' was also raised. It was recommended that this should include operating within the local community i.e. becoming a community resource, as well as access to our courses.

2.1.3   With reference to the key messages in *Official Channel*, the view was put forward that members of the University community do not feel knowledgeable about the University's overall academic strategy. Thus a more realistic objective might be for members of the community to understand the role which they play in the overall scheme of things. The University's priorities will only be achieved through the efforts of its staff. Therefore, careful thought needs to be given to the means by which the goals, the means of achieving them and progress against targets is communicated to the staff. An organisational framework for planning is needed to enable achievements towards the overall strategic objectives to take place on the ground. This should form part of the planning process. The revised Strategic Plan would require a fresh marketing strategy.

2.1.4　In terms of processes it was commented that there needs to be review of activities as well as development or further development of strategies and plans. Also when implementing plans it is important not to overlook the means by which that is done since this can impact on the community e.g. environmental issues. The means will give an impression of the values to which we ascribe.

2.1.5　There were additional comments about improving communication and sharing to help foster a community and for mutual benefit. For example, we could share information on partners and links; provide support and advice on how to build external partnerships and links. Excellent contacts have been made by some individual members of the University with outside organisations including international and European links. Now perhaps the time has come to commission an overview, to have institutional ownership and to be selective, where necessary. In a similar vein it was acknowledged that faculties should have individual identities but that this should not inhibit inter-faculty cooperation and working.

2.1.6　In relation to collaboration with other institutions, the value of two-way secondments was recognised. The need to liaise better with colleagues doing similar things in other institutions was raised. In terms of the definition of our region, we should not be lured into focusing only on the 'coastal strip'. The region may mean different things in different contexts. Further it is believed that there is no conflict in the University simultaneously having regional and international aspirations.

2.1.7　In terms of academic frameworks to deliver the plan, emphasis on simplification and strengthening modular provision was recommended. Also doing away with the servicing model was stressed as a means of enabling and incentivising inter-faculty collaboration.

2.1.8　There were suggestions for additions or amendments to the strategic priorities including:

- improving performance in generic research and intellectual property rights;
- including learning and teaching in the sub-section on academic structures and portfolio;
- adding the social, cultural and sports aspects as important to the quality of the students' experience;
- even more emphasis needs to be given to part-time provision.

2.2　Senior staff seminars

2.2.1　At the seminars Deans and Heads presented their vision for the area for which they have responsibility. During this a number of key issues emerged which are relevant to the production of the Strategic Plan and/or the operating objectives derived from it.

2.2.2　A common theme which emerged was the need for a better understanding of standards and expectations across the University. One of the original strategic priorities in the consultation paper was 'to enhance our academic portfolio so that more of what we offer is at the same standard and quality as its current best elements'. However, following discussion, this is more likely to be put in terms of differential goals for different parts of the portfolio. The implementation issue then is how we respect and reward these differential goals; i.e. how to have differential goals within a shared vision. Of relevance therefore is the means of achieving strong cohesive schools while at the same time delivering University priorities including inter-faculty working. In parallel with that is the role of central departments, how best use is made of them and how their plans relate to the Strategic Plan.

2.2.3 The articulation of standards and expectations hinges on a balancing act, between different ends of various spectra:

- individual autonomy and community;
- diversification and concentration;
- quality and increased access;
- local, national and international priorities.

A shared notion of how to make judgements about where to position different areas on the spectra is important, as well as respect for the differing positions which emerge.

2.2.4 The seminar also focused on a number of case studies which also triggered some issues. Most of these related directly or indirectly to the establishment of good infrastructure, with, for example, the following purposes:

- to provide information necessary to ensure plans can be rigorously analysed;
- to provide a strategic approach to communications at all levels with different members of the University community;
- if the academic portfolio is to be reviewed, to provide criteria and parameters for the review.

2.2.5 The importance of good communication channels was raised from different perspectives: to network between those with similar responsibility across the University; to enable central departments to be proactive rather than reactive; externally to improve our corporate image.

3 Key points arising from the responses of external partners

Where the responses raised issues of relevance to the draft of the University's planning process, the key points are summarised below group by group.

(i) Observations:

- the correct identification in the analysis of the changing environment of the likely priorities of the new government, particularly the emphasis on increasing access for currently underrepresented and socially excluded people.

Omissions:

- under the strategic priority relating to paying attention to the whole student experience, the possibility of working with Brighton & Hove Council and the private sector to ensure a high standard of accommodation for students;
- the need to minimise the use of private transport in favour of bus and train;
- emphasis on the region i.e. the South-East as opposed to Sussex.

(ii) ## Observations:

- apparently less emphasis than in previous plans on diversification and maximisation of funding;
- the possibilities for associating with similar institutions overseas for collaboration, joint preparation of learning materials and benchmarking of standards;
- the opportunity for the University to define its 'region' and correspondingly enlarge the academic corridor.

Omissions:

- strategic partnerships with business (public and private) for joint provision including accreditation;
- targets for academic success e.g. relating to professional and vocational success of graduates;
- building further on the University's pioneering work in Europe.

(iii) ## Support for:

- flexible modes of delivery and development of research portfolio;
- Academic Corridor project as an important initiative to help broaden the economy of the area;
- valued contribution to regeneration activity;
- the possibility of collaboration with FE colleges, Sussex Enterprise, etc. to address local skills shortages;
- continuing the University's particular strength in professional and vocational work;
- the concept of the University as an exemplar in its role as an employer with particular emphasis on Investors in People recognition.

Observations:

- district councils could usefully be included in the list of key partners by referring to the Councils of East and West Sussex rather than listing specific councils;
- a cross-boundary approach to CPD particularly valuable with the likely emphasis on working across agencies providing health and social care;
- the potential to work with employers in high level skills development is likely to grow;

- the need to be increasingly proactive in building understanding at all levels of the University of the modern commercial and industrial needs.

Omissions:
- environmental, sustainable development and Local Agenda 21 issues;
- the strategic significance of Newhaven as one of the areas for social and economic development.

(iv) *Support for:*
- the focus on partnerships and also Europe.

Observations:
- the emphasis in the plan of the supply side, for example, on 'education' rather than 'learning'.
- now might be opportune to establish an Endowment Committee to develop appropriate vehicles to ensure for example that donations are used in a tax-efficient way.

Omissions:
- an emphasis on guidance for learners to make the most of learning opportunities;
- making more of the University's sub-region, for example, to reflect the increased tendency for undergraduate students to study locally, the increased emphasis on lifelong learning and CPD, the research and development and income potential offered by local industrial links;
- the importance of enhancing employment prospects for graduates.

(v) *Observations:*
Partnership with the FE sector could include:

- University for Industry;
- HNC/D course development;
- shared delivery of courses with joint delivery;
- integrate entry courses more closely with University provision;
- joint staff development programmes.

Further desirable developments:
- extension of the Academic Corridor to the Worthing area;
- collaboration between West Sussex schools and colleges and Academic Corridor members.

Omissions:
- specific mention of Lewes and Newhaven in the reference to the potential for the University with its partners to make a positive impact on the economic development of the region;
- the possible development of a medical school;
- greater emphasis on opportunities for developing multi-professional training of health professionals.

4   The way forward

4.1   There are obviously some recurrent themes from both the internal and external consultation which will get played into the draft of the Strategic Plan, which will be produced in July 1998. The revised timetable for the production of the Plan agreed by the Board will allow the Plan to take into account announcements expected this summer on the Government's Comprehensive Spending Review and on other initiatives such as the role of Regional Development Agencies.

4.2   The following stages are proposed for the planning process.

(i)   Strategic Plan

This will consist of two parts. The first will be aimed at a wide variety of audiences and will set out the University's common purpose, mission and vision. It is intended to be a clear statement of how the University of Brighton sees itself and its sense of direction for the five year period up to 2003 and beyond, depending on the external environment. It will also include:

- our broad strategy i.e. high level priorities;
- major internal and external factors impacting on the University;
- long-term aims.

The second part will comprise a detailed set of operational objectives derived from the high level priorities. It will contain the main means by which the priorities will be implemented and will have associated measurable targets. This is intended to be a working document for the University community and the Board of Governors. The objectives will be kept under continual review most likely with a rolling three year horizon. It will contain as an appendix the maintenance of the Plan and a schedule for the regular annual planning cycle including the development of the financial forecast, annual operating statement and review (see (ii) and (iii) below).

(ii)   Annual operating statement

This will be produced each year for the subsequent financial year. It will include goals, deadlines, responsibilities and targets to be achieved over the next financial year, as a measure of performance. The operating goals would be annual milestones on the road to achieving our five year operational objectives.

(iii)   Review of progress against targets in the operating statement

During and at the end of each financial year progress against the goals as set out in the current annual operating statement will be reviewed.

At the end of the year, any significant difference between actual performance and the goals and targets as set out on the operating statement will be analysed and discussed. As a result the five year operational objectives might be updated.

4.3   It has already been agreed that, with the changes to the organisation of the University, there will be a greater emphasis on planning at faculty and school level, and this should link with the corporate planning process. The plans of the central support departments, offices and units will also fit into this process.

4.4 There are two dimensions to the involvement of faculties, schools and central departments:

(a) to ensure a sense of ownership of the corporate level plans by the members of the University community via consultation;

(b) the production of local plans which are consistent with and feed into the corporate level plans; the aggregated local plans will provide the detail behind the main proposals for the implementation of the corporate plans.

4.5 The schedule for the planning process will enable activities (a) and (b) to be undertaken in parallel. There would be consultation on the draft Strategic Plan during that time. This could also be used as the stimulus for faculties, schools and central departments to start the production of their own plans, or to revise their existing plans where relevant. By this process any potential mismatches or omissions between the corporate level operational objectives and 'local' plans could emerge.

4.6 A timetable for the production of the Strategic Plan is presented in Appendix 1. The Plan will be presented for approval to the Board at its meeting in December 1998. This will permit further consultation within the University prior to presentation to the Academic Board in November.

Head of Strategic Planning Unit   15.6.98

Appendix 1   Timetable for the production of the Strategic Plan

by end of July 1998	Production of draft of Strategic Plan v1.
5 October	Management Group discussion of Strategic Plan v1 particularly the proposed targets. Further amendments to produce v2.
early Autumn Term	Revised draft of Strategic Plan v2 to be considered at Faculty Management Groups and central department meetings of senior staff in these departments to seek feedback and also to initiate discussion on local plans.
4 November	Feedback to Management Forum (Directorate, Deans and Heads) of local discussions on Strategic Plan so far. Strategic Plan to be revised (v3).

Appendix 1   *(cont'd)*

12 November	Academic Development Committee receives latest draft of Strategic Plan v3 prior to final draft being produced for Academic Board (v4).
9, 11, 13, 18 November Faculty Boards Central department meetings	Faculty boards and central departments receive v3 of Strategic Plan to start to consider the approval of local plans.
26 November	Academic Board receives v4 of Strategic Plan for approval. Minor amendments to produce v5.
11 December	Board of Governors receives v5 for final approval.
mid December	Publication of Strategic Plan 1999–2004.
January 1999	Open meetings to communicate with the University community about the Plan.

Document 4

Corporate Plan 1999–2004
The University of Brighton's mission

The University of Brighton is dedicated to the discovery of new knowledge, the testing of received knowledge and the creative, responsible and effective application of knowledge. It seeks to be an accessible, dynamic and responsive community of higher education with special strengths in professional and vocational education, applied research and consultancy.

The University's underlying aims are to

- maintain the best of the values of its history while introducing new features in response to fresh challenges
- develop an academic portfolio which combines flexibility of response to changing external demand with assured quality
- continue to collaborate with selected regional, national and international partners on a basis of mutual benefit and respect
- improve continuously the environment in which members of the community study, work and live

Shared values

The University re-affirms the values which have informed its work since its foundation:

- not to discriminate unfairly either directly or indirectly against members or prospective members of the community
- to acknowledge and value corporate independence and to accept the responsibilities and rights it embodies
- to value freedom of thought and its appropriate expression
- to encourage the participation of members of the university community in its corporate activities and its decision making processes
- to support the personal and professional development of all members of the community

Strategy for 1999–2004

The strategy for 1999–2004 focuses on five key areas:

- academic structures and portfolio;
- quality assurance and systems;

- support for members of the university;
- partnerships and community role;
- governance and infrastructure.

Strategic Area A: academic portfolio and structures

Background

The University's academic portfolio consists of an overlapping and mutually reinforcing range of activities: full and part-time undergraduate programmes; postgraduate, post-experience and continuing vocational education courses; liberal adult education; services to business, industry and other public services; and applied and basic research. The academic portfolio is soundly based and has significant strengths (see also Strategic Area B). Further modernisation is needed in response to new challenges.

The University remains committed to organising its academic provision through a small number of faculties focusing on its major subject areas: paramedical; science; engineering and built environment; computing, mathematics and information management; business management; applied social science; languages; initial and in-service teacher training; and art and design including their history and cultural aspects. Understanding of and expertise in methods of learning and teaching are regarded as indispensable for all those concerned with course development and delivery.

Future challenges

Increasing participation and lifelong learning are being prioritised by Government. Plans have been announced to fund 80,000 extra places in higher education by 2001/02, with 35,000 of these (up to 20,000 part-time) in 1999/2000, enabling universities to play a full part in these initiatives. To foster a culture of lifelong learning it is necessary for our courses to accommodate a range of learners with different aspirations.

National Education and Training Targets include the goal of 28% of the workforce having a vocational, management or academic qualification at NVQ Level 4 or above by 2002. The establishment of a highly trained workforce will depend on upgrading individuals' skills and raising attainment at all levels including through higher education programmes.

The development of a national qualifications framework and an underpinning credit framework by the Quality Assurance Agency (QAA) will influence academic development work and lead to a rationalisation of award titles. The potential of the academic portfolio to develop to meet these requirements will depend on the flexibility of the academic framework for curricula and awards, and on collaboration between faculties.

The next Research Assessment Exercise (RAE) will take place in 2001. In the Comprehensive Spending Review (CSR) funds are being released over the next three year period for a major boost to research, including refurbishment of laboratories and replacement of equipment.

Priorities for 1999–2004

- the University's main goal is to maintain and enhance the quality and relevance of its academic programmes in teaching, research and services to business and the community
- to establish appropriate goals for each part of the University
- to adjust the academic portfolio as necessary to ensure that it meets the needs of current and potential students, as well as of employers; by revising courses, agreeing patterns of growth and contraction, and promoting inter-faculty collaboration
- to contribute to the national priorities of widening participation and life-long learning
- to simplify, where possible, academic frameworks, academic regulations and awards titles
- to develop further the research strategy including the identification of new funding streams

Strategic Area B: quality assurance and quality systems

Background

The latest round of funding council teaching quality assessments/subject reviews has resulted in strong results (all either 3 or 4 out of a possible 4) in each of the assessed areas. The Office for Standards in Education (OFSTED) inspections of the initial teacher training provision, in both secondary and primary, have also produced extremely positive outcomes. Well developed procedures for assuring and auditing quality are in place.

In the Research Assessment Exercise undertaken by the funding council in 1996, members of the University improved their score in 11 of the 20 units submitted. Two units had lower scores than in 1992. Competitive research grant successes have been achieved in key areas, consultancy has continued to expand, and substantial industrial sponsorships have been obtained.

While the overall picture is sound, the quality of some provision is less strong and the embedding of procedures is variable. The transfer of good practice from areas of acknowledged strength to those in need of further development is an important objective.

To reflect the value which the University places on development of expertise in methods of learning and teaching, a policy for the accreditation of all teaching staff has been agreed. The University is reviewing quality measures and procedures and investigating the applicability of the Investors in People (IIP) programme.

Future challenges

The report of the National Committee of Inquiry into Higher Education published in 1997 identified the need for firmer measures to safeguard standards and for enhanced professionalism in teaching. The former is being taken forward through the work of the QAA and the latter through the

Institute of Learning and Teaching (ILT). While our core systems and processes are currently sound, they will have to evolve to take account of the changes. In particular, the University must ensure that its students taught in partner institutions in the UK and overseas benefit from the same careful approach to quality assurance as students studying within the University.

Priorities for 1999–2004

- to sustain demonstrable academic standards and quality of student educational experience through high-quality teaching and learning support, and to seek further developments and improvements where necessary, including by supporting accreditation of staff by the ILT
- to play a full and constructive part in the further development of national quality assurance and accreditation frameworks for UK higher education via creative and critical participation in the work of national agencies and professional and statutory bodies
- to refine and implement more clearly processes for enabling and monitoring high quality achievement by research groups and research students
- to develop a quality strategy covering academic and support service processes, and human and physical resources, including special accommodation and equipment needs
- to establish systems and procedures to enable members of the University to monitor performance and to provide a high quality service

Strategic Area C: support for members of the University community

Background

The University is conscious that its chief asset supporting its academic goals is the intellectual capital of its staff and students. Consequently, it is committed to the development of all its staff and to the provision of a high quality experience for its students.

The University's policy on staff development makes development and training an integral part of the working life of each member of staff. This is associated with both an individual's own personal and professional development and training, and the requirements of the University's strategic plan.

The annual review of academic health also reviews elements of pastoral and other support for students.

Marked progress has been made on developing information services, communication networks and the physical environment in support of the whole university community.

Future challenges

As an employer the University is committed to encouraging and supporting the lifelong learning agenda for all of its staff, and will refresh and extend its staff development practices and plans.

The introduction of tuition fees for full-time undergraduate students and the expansion of loan and access funds requires additional advice and support for students.

The University of Brighton is unusual in having a number of significantly sized campuses, being neither a single campus-based institution nor one with a main site and small satellites. This presents particular challenges to ensure the recognition and support of a common organisational culture.

Priorities for 1999–2004

- to nurture and develop the institution's intellectual capital
- to support members of the university community by being careful of their working conditions and of the quality of their working lives
- to identify the further needs of the University's communities for training and staff development and to ensure that provision is in place to meet those needs
- to consider all aspects of students' experience and the means of delivering a high quality experience including learning resources, student services, guidance and support, studying and living arrangements, part-time employment and social, cultural and sports activities
- to operate with sensitivity to environmental and sustainability issues
- to develop a formal information strategy and to improve the internal and external communications network
- to develop and increase the presence of the arts, sport and recreation across the whole university

Strategic Area D: partnerships and community role

Background

Strong links have been established with key local and regional players, including: higher and further education institutions; local authorities; schools; health authorities and trusts; local and regional arts bodies; local and regional economic and community development organisations; and government departments, including the Government Office for the South East (GOSE).

The University has extensive partnerships with businesses and industry sector groups, including those supporting research, consultancy, professional development, undergraduate and postgraduate courses and placements.

The University has agreed an international statement which guides an active strategy of internationalism; as a result, a wide range of international partnerships has been established.

Future challenges

A significant challenge to all education institutions in the early twenty-first century will be to collaborate and to form local and regional partnerships.

From the existing sound base the University will further develop mature working relationships with existing partners and seek to develop arrangements with new partners, including the new South East England Development Agency (SEEDA), for mutual economic, social and educational benefit.

The University needs to establish a better definition of its region and the sub-regions served by its campuses, and to make more of their potential, for example, to reflect: the increased tendency for undergraduate students to study locally; the research and development potential offered by local and regional public and private sectors; and the increased emphasis on lifelong learning and continuing professional development (CPD).

Priorities for 1999–2004

- to collaborate constructively and selectively with local and regional partners to influence beneficially local and regional educational, economic and social development, including by encouraging participation from all sectors of the community, and to achieve a national reputation as a significant local and regional player
- to develop further the collaborative partnerships with: SEEDA; GOSE; Sussex Enterprise; Business Link; local authorities; educational partners; professional and statutory bodies; the NHS consortia responsible for commissioning education and training; health trusts; regional arts bodies; businesses, especially the small and medium sized enterprise (SME) sector; and relevant community groups
- to define our 'region' and correspondingly extend the 'Academic Corridor' as an important initiative in support of the regional economy
- to develop further the partnerships and framework needed for the effective exploitation of research and development
- to continue to play a constructive international and European role in collaboration with selected partners

Strategic Area E: governance and infrastructure

Background

The University became an independent higher education corporation in 1989. Its Board of Governors has provided strong and effective leadership, focusing on its key tasks of determining the educational character and mission of the University, ensuring its solvency, and providing the policy framework within which the University is managed. Academic governance has been carried forward through the Academic Board and its committee structure.

Under the Board of Governors' leadership, the University has developed a financial position that is relatively strong compared to the HE sector as a whole. The University has faced successive reductions in public funding per student and continuing requirements to redevelop the University's products and environment. This means that the financial strategy must be regularly reviewed to ensure that resources are available to enable the University's strategic and operational objectives to be achieved.

A great deal of progress has been made in the implementation of the Estate Strategy published in 1995. However significant projects remain to be completed, notably at the Eastbourne, Falmer and Grand Parade campuses.

Future challenges

The effectiveness of the governance framework needs testing against the expectations set out in the report of the National Committee of Inquiry into Higher Education, the Committee of Standards in Public Life, and the Higher Education Funding Council for England (HEFCE).

In order to maximise income, it is essential that all activity is based upon sound market research and analysis and a focused plan for promotion. In addition it is essential that a holistic approach is taken to the provision of services to existing corporate clients. New sources of income must also be identified and exploited, in particular through the application of knowledge to address business problems, particularly those of small and medium sized enterprises.

Public funding for estates development remains very limited. In order to achieve targets it will be necessary to find innovative ways of developing and improving facilities, including in partnership with the public and private sectors.

Priorities for 1999–2004

- to conduct an initial review of governance, and to develop a framework for a regular review and reporting process
- to develop further the University's financial strategy in support of its academic goals and to continue its effective financial management
- to develop a marketing strategy and to ensure that all activity is based on sound market intelligence and has a focused plan for promotion
- to continue the development of the quality of the working environment to benefit the University's community

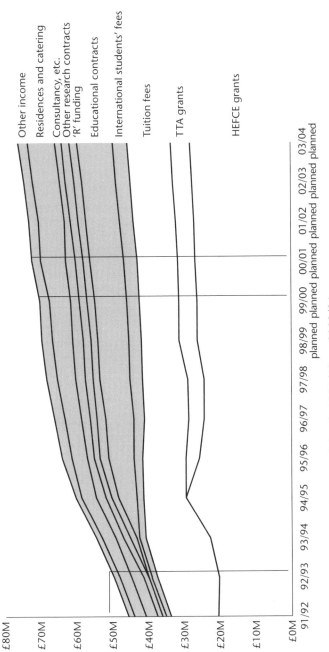

Document 4, Figure 1 Sources of funds 1991/92 to 2003/04

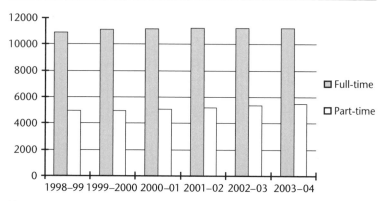

Document 4, Figure 2 Student number plans 1998/99 to 2003/04

REFERENCES

Aaronovitch, D. (1998) Could poverty lead students to prostitution and drug dealing?, *Independent*, 4 June, p. 21.

Advisory Board for the Research Councils (ABRC) (1987) *A Strategy for the Science Base*. London: HMSO.

Aitkin, D. (1998) What do Vice-chancellors do? *Journal of Higher Education Policy and Management*, 20(2): 117–28.

Anon (1998) Prinny writes . . . , *University of Sussex Bulletin*, 13 February.

Ashby, E. (1958) *Technology and the Academics: An Essay on Universities and the Scientific Revolution*. London: Macmillan.

Association of Heads of University Administration (AHUA) (1999) *Corporate Governance in Universities: Report on Survey of Activity*. Norwich: AHUA Governance Group.

Association for University and College Counselling (AUCC) (1999) *Degrees of Disturbance: The New Agenda – The Impact of Increasing Levels of Psychological Disturbance Amongst Students in Higher Education*. Rugby: British Association for Counselling.

Barnes, B. (1985) *About Science*. Oxford: Blackwell.

Barnett, R. (1990) *The Idea of Higher Education*. Milton Keynes: SRHE and Open University Press.

Barnett, R. (1994) *The Limits of Competence: Knowledge, Higher Education and Society*. Buckingham: SRHE and Open University Press.

Barnett, R. (1997) *Higher Education: A Critical Business*. Buckingham: SRHE and Open University Press.

Becher, T. (1989) *Academic Tribes and Territories: Intellectual Inquiry and the Cultures of Disciplines*. Milton Keynes: SRHE and Open University Press.

Bennell, P. (1998) with T. Pearce, *The Internationalisation of Higher Education: Exporting Education to Developing and Transitional Economies*, working paper no. 75. Sussex: Institute of Development Studies.

Berlant, L. (1998) Collegiality, Crisis and Cultural Studies, *Profession 1998*, 105–16.

Berlin, I. (1969) *Four Essays on Liberty*. Oxford and New York: Oxford University Press.

Berry, C. (1999) University league tables: artefacts and inconsistencies in individual rankings, *Higher Education Review*, 31(2): 3–10.

Billinghurst, B. (1995) No sex please, we're tutors, *Times Higher Education Supplement*, 30 June: 12.

Bourgeois, E. (1991) Dependence, legitimation and power in academic decision-making, *Higher Education Policy*, 4(2): 21–3.

Bowman, C. and Asch, D. (1996) *Managing Strategy*. Basingstoke: Macmillan Business.

Bristow, J. (1995) Teachers and petting do mix, *Times Higher Education Supplement*, 2 June: 12.

Browning, G. (1999) Office politics, *Guardian Weekend*, 27 February.

Bruce, A. (1999) Setting boundaries for strategic management, *Professional Manager*, 8(1): 8–10.

Campbell, K. and Bryceland, C. (1998) *Policing the Campus: Providing a Safe and Secure Environment*. London: Home Office Police Policy Directorate.

Cardiff University (1998) To be a world class university . . . , *Cardiff News*, October.

Chan, S.S. (1993) Changing roles of institutional research in strategic management, *Research in Higher Education*, 34(5): 533–49.

Charter, D. (1995) Lecturers told to dampen ardour, *Times Higher Education Supplement*, 2 June: 4.

Clare, J. (1998) University judged not competent to award degrees, *Daily Telegraph*, 13 November.

Clark, B.R. (1998) *Creating Entrepreneurial Universities: Organizational Pathways of Transformation*. Oxford: Pergamon for IAU Press.

Committee of University Chairmen (CUC) (1998) *Guide for Members of Governing Bodies of Universities and Colleges in England, Wales and Northern Ireland*. Bristol: Higher Education Funding Council for England, External Relations.

Committee of Vice-Chancellors and Principals (CVCP) (1985) *Efficiency in Universities*, report of the Steering Committee for Efficiency Studies in Universities, the 'Jarratt Report'. London: CVCP.

Committee of Vice-Chancellors and Principals (CVCP) (1994) *Universities and Communities*. London: CVCP.

Committee of Vice-Chancellors and Principals (CVCP) (1998a) *CVCP Corporate Plan 1998/2001*. London: CVCP.

Committee of Vice-Chancellors and Principals (CVCP) (1998b) *CVCP Submission to the Comprehensive Spending Review*, 1/98/38(a).

Committee of Vice-Chancellors and Principals (CVCP) (1998c) *Extremism and Intolerance on Campus*. London: CVCP.

Coopers and Lybrand (1998) *Indirect Costs of OST Research Council Projects and Programmes*. Unpublished report commissioned by the Committee of Vice-Chancellors and Principals, the Higher Education Funding Council for England, and the Office of Science & Technology.

Coulson-Thomas, C. and Coe, T. (1991) *The Flat Organisation: Philosophy and Practice*. Corby: British Institute of Management.

Council for Industry and Higher Education (CIHE) (1997) *CIHE's Response to Higher Education in the Learning Society, the Report of the National Committee of Inquiry into Higher Education.* London: CIHE.

Cuthbert, R. (ed.) (1996) *Working in Higher Education.* Buckingham: SRHE and Open University Press.

Dearing, R. (1998) *The 1998 University of Westminster International Education Lecture: A Lecture by Lord Dearing.* International Lecture Series, University of Westminster, 8 May. London: University of Westminster.

Deem, R. (1998a) New managerialism in higher education: the management of performance and cultures in universities, *International Studies in the Sociology of Education*, 8(1): 47–70.

Deem, R. (1998b) Managing universities of the future: new managerialism, new public service management and femocracies. Unpublished plenary presentation to 'Higher Education Close Up' Conference, Preston, 7 July.

Department for Education and Employment (DfEE) (1998a) *The Learning Age: A Renaissance for a New Britain*, Green Paper. London: HMSO.

Department for Education and Employment (DfEE) (1998b) *Higher Education for the 21st Century: A Response to the Dearing Report.* London: HMSO.

Department for Education and Employment (DfEE) (1998c) *Further Education for the New Millennium: A Response to the Kennedy Report.* London: HMSO.

Department for Education and Employment (DfEE) (1998d) *Prior Options Review of the Higher Education Funding Council for England: Questions to Interested Organisations.* London: DfEE.

Department for Education and Employment (DfEE) (1998e) £19 billion boost for education, DfEE Press Release 360/98, 14 July.

Department for Education and Employment (DfEE) (1998f) Higher education funding for 1999–00 and beyond, Letter to Chief Executive of HEFCE, 8 December.

Department for Education and Employment (DfEE) (1998g) *Towards a National Skills Agenda. First Report of the National Skills Task Force.* London: HMSO.

Department for Education and Employment (DfEE) (1998h) *Labour Market and Skill Trends 1998/99.* Suffolk: DfEE.

Dworkin, R. (1996) We need a new interpretation of academic freedom, in L. Menand (ed.) *The Future of Academic Freedom.* Chicago and London: University of Chicago Press.

Easterby-Smith, M. (1987) Change and innovation in higher education: a role for corporate strategy? *Higher Education*, 16(1): 37–52.

Edge Hill (1998) *Strategic Plan Summary, 1998–1999.* Edge Hill University College.

Ehrenberg, R.G. (1999) Adam Smith goes to college: an economist becomes an academic administrator, *Journal of Economic Perspectives,* 13(1): 99–116.

Farnham, D. and Jones, J. (1998) Who are the vice chancellors? An analysis of their professional and social backgrounds, 1990–97, *Higher Education Review*, 30(3): 42–58.

Fisher, S. (1994) *Stress in Academic Life: the Mental Assembly Line.* Buckingham: SRHE and Open University Press.

Fryer, R.H. (1997) *Learning for the Twenty-First Century.* First Report of the National Advisory Group for Continuing Education and Lifelong Learning. London: HMSO.

Gibson, J. (1998) Students work in sex clubs to fund courses, *Independent*, 8 June: 8.

Gilliat-Ray, S. (1999) *Higher Education and Student Religious Identity*. Exeter: University of Exeter and the Inter Faith Network for the UK.

Glion Colloquium (1998) *The Glion Declaration: the University at the Millennium*. Switzerland: Glion.

Goleman, D. (1998) What makes a leader? *Harvard Business Review*, November–December: 93–102.

Grier, J. and Johns, A. (1998) *Time for lunch: managing stress at work*. Good Practice Series Number 21. Manchester: Association of University Administrators.

Gwyther, M. (1999) Stresses for success, *Management Today*, January: 22–6.

Halpin, T. (1998) Failed university that can't even count its students, *Daily Mail*, 13 November: 17.

Harvey, L. (1999) The sense in satisfaction, *Times Higher Education Supplement*, 15 January: 29.

Harvey, L. with Plimmer, L., Moon, S. and Geall, V. (1997) *Student Satisfaction Manual*. Buckingham: SRHE and Open University Press.

Health and Safety Executive (HSE) (1998) *Annual Report and Accounts, 1997/1998*. London: HSE.

Higher Education Funding Council for England (HEFCE) (1998a) *1998–2001 Corporate Plan*, Report 98/23. Bristol: HEFCE.

Higher Education Funding Council for England (HEFCE) (1998b) *Analysis of 1997 Strategic Plans*, Report 98/07. Bristol: HEFCE.

Higher Education Funding Council for England (HEFCE) (1998c) *Appraising Investment Decisions: Draft for Consultation*, Consultation 98/55. Bristol: HEFCE.

Higher Education Funding Council for England (HEFCE) (1998d) *Audit by the HEFCE*, Guide 98/64. Bristol: HEFCE.

Higher Education Funding Council for England (HEFCE) (1998e) *Effective Financial Management in Higher Education: A Guide for Governors, Heads of Institution and Senior Managers*, Report 98/29. Bristol: HEFCE.

Higher Education Funding Council for England (HEFCE) (1998f) *Institutions' Corporate Plans*, Consultation 98/13. Bristol: HEFCE.

Higher Education Funding Council for England (HEFCE) (1998g) *How the HEFCE Promotes Value for Money*, Guide 98/63. Bristol: HEFCE.

Higher Education Funding Council for England (HEFCE) (1998h), HEFCE announces action plan for Thames Valley University, Press Release, 12 November.

Higher Education Funding Council for England (HEFCE) (1999a) *HEFCE Strategic Plan 1999–2004*, Report 99/31. Bristol: HEFCE.

Higher Education Funding Council for England (HEFCE) (1999b) *Corporate Planning*, Circular Letter 3/99. Bristol: HEFCE.

Higher Education Funding Council for England (HEFCE) (1999c) *1999 Annual Operating Statement, Planning Return and Financial Forecasts*, Request 99/30. Bristol: HEFCE.

Higher Education Funding Council for England (HEFCE) (1999d) *Performance Indicators in Higher Education: First Report of the Performance Indicators Steering Group*, Report 99/11. Bristol: HEFCE.

Higher Education Funding Council for England (HEFCE) (1999e) *Estate Management Statistics Project*, Report 99/18. Bristol: HEFCE.

Higher Education Funding Council for England (HEFCE) (1999f) *Institutional Learning and Teaching Strategies: A Guide to Good Practice*, Good Practice Guide 99/55. Bristol: HEFCE.

Higher Education Funding Council for England (HEFCE) (forthcoming) *Strategic Planning in the HE Sector: A Guide for Governors, Heads of Institutions and Senior Managers*. Bristol: HEFCE.

Hodges, L. (1998) Cannabis on campus – repression is no answer, *Independent: Education*, 21 May: 2–3.

House, D. and Watson, D. (1995) Managing change, in D. Warner and E. Crosthwaite (eds) *Human Resource Management in Higher and Further Education*. Buckingham: SRHE and Open University Press.

Kelly, N.H. and Shaw, R.N. (1987) Strategic planning by academic institutions – following the corporate path? *Higher Education*, 16(3): 319–36.

Kennedy, H. (1997) *Learning Works: Widening Participation in Further Education*. Coventry: FEFC.

Kingston University (1998) Commission on the Future of Kingston University, *Bridge*, 12, October: 1–2.

Klein, J. (1998) The town that ate itself: Washington's politics of self-destruction, *The New Yorker*, 23 November: 78–87.

Knight, P. and Harvey, L. (1999) The use of a staff satisfaction survey at the University of Central England in Birmingham, *Perspectives: Policy and Practice in Higher Education*, 3(2): 56–62.

Korac-Kakabadse, A., Korac-Kakabadese, N. and Myers, A. (1998) Demographics and leadership philosophy: exploring gender differences, *Journal of Management Development*, 17(5): 351–88.

Kular, R. and Winn, S. (1998) *The Financial Situation of Students at the University of Brighton: The Seventh Report, 1997–98*. University of Brighton: Health and Social Policy Research Centre.

Lacey, H. (1998) Stressed? Relaxation is not the answer, *Independent on Sunday*, 24 May: 26.

Lawson, I. (1999) *Leaders for Tomorrow's Society*. London: Industrial Society.

Lindsay, R. (1987) Modular Course Staff Survey, *Teaching News* 17, Spring: 12–15. Oxford: Oxford Polytechnic.

Lockwood, G. and Davies, J. (1985) *Universities: the Management Challenge*. Windsor: SRHE and NFER-Nelson.

Ma, K. (1999) Business and academic leaders disagree on how colleges should be run, *Chronicle of Higher Education*, 20 January.

MacIntyre, A. (1993) Are philosophical problems insoluble? The relevance of system and history, in P. Cook (ed.) *Philosophical Imagination and Cultural Memory: Appropriating Historical Tradition*. Durham and London: Duke University Press.

Major, L.E. (1998) Watch out, Whitehall, *Guardian: Higher Education*, 10 November: ii–iii.

Marshall, A. (1890) *Principles of Economics*. London: Macmillan.

Marshall, J. (1998) The globe warms to further study, *Times Higher Education Supplement*, 27 November: 14.

Mason, D. (1998) *Management and Administrative Computing Initiative: Post-implementation Review – Summary Report*. Bristol: JISC.

Meade, P.H. (1997) *Challenges Facing Universities: Quality, Leadership and the Management of Change*. Dunedin, New Zealand: University of Otago.

Middlehurst, R. (1993) *Leading Academics*. Buckingham: SRHE and Open University Press.

Moore, J.L. (1992) *Writers on Strategy and Strategic Management: The Theory of Strategy and the Practice of Strategic Management at Enterprise, Corporate, Business and Functional Levels*. London: Penguin Books.

National Association of Teachers in Further and Higher Education (NATFHE) (1998) New era of partnership needed at TVU, Press Release, 13 November.

National Audit Office (NAO) (1998) *Investigation of Misconduct at Glasgow Caledonian University*. London: HMSO.

National Committee of Inquiry into Higher Education (NCIHE) (1997) *Higher Education in the Learning Society: Main Report*. London: HMSO.

Neave, G. (1998) Growing Pains: The Dearing Report from a European Perspective, *Higher Education Quarterly*, 52(1): 118–36.

Nie, N., Junn, J. and Stehlik-Barry, K. (1996) *Education and Democratic Citizenship in America*. Chicago, Ill.: University of Chicago Press.

Office of Population Censuses and Surveys, Social Survey Division (OPCS) (1995) *Qualified Nurses, Midwives and Health Visitors*. London: HMSO.

Organization for Economic Cooperation Development (OECD) (1998) *Education at a Glance: OECD Indicators 1998*. Paris: OECD.

Pinto, R. (1996) *Social Business*. The Newchurch Lecture Series. London: Newchurch and Company.

Pratt, J. (1997) *The Polytechnic Experiment, 1965–92*. Buckingham: SRHE and Open University Press.

Quality Assurance Agency (QAA) (1998a) Thames Valley University: 'standards at risk' says agency, Press Release, 12 November.

Quality Assurance Agency (QAA) (1998b) *Special Review of Thames Valley University*. Gloucester: QAA.

Quality Assurance Agency (QAA) (1999) *Review of the Criteria for Degree Awarding Powers and University Title*. Gloucester: QAA.

Radford, J., Raaheim, K., de Vries, P. and Williams, R. (1997) *Quantity and Quality in Higher Education*. London: Jessica Kingsley.

Rauch, J. (1993) *Kindly Inquisitors: The New Attacks on Free Thought*. Chicago and London: University of Chicago Press.

Rhodes, F.H.T. (1998) The art of the presidency, *The Presidency* (American Council on Education), 1(1): 12–19.

Richards, S. (1997) Promoting change through public policy, *RSA Journal*, CLV: 5478 (April): 31–7.

Rittel, H. and Webber, M.M. (1973) Dilemmas in a general theory of planning, *Policy Sciences*, 4: 155–69.

Robertson, D. (1999) Soapbox, *Times Higher Education Supplement*, 15 January: 16.

Rolnick, J. (1998) Wesleyan's 'Independent Ivy' campaign elicits a sour response from students, *Chronicle of Higher Education*, 14 October.

Rorty, R. (1998) *Achieving Our Country*. Cambridge and London: Harvard University Press.

Royal Society for the encouragement of Arts, Manufacture and Commerce (RSA) (1998) Is there a crisis in leadership? *RSA Journal*, 5486(3): 74–80.

Salford University (1998) The Way Ahead, *Update* 47, 12 October.

Sarah Lawrence (1998) Michele Tolela Myers inaugurated ninth President of Sarah Lawrence College, Press Release, 25 September.

Schuller, T. (1998) Social capital and community-building, in K. Hurley (ed.) *University Continuing Education in Partnership for Development. UACE Annual Conference 1997, Proceedings*. Leeds: UACE.

Scott, P. (1995) *The Meanings of Mass Higher Education*. Buckingham: SRHE and Open University Press.

Scott, P. (ed.) (1998) *The Globalization of Higher Education*. Buckingham: SRHE and Open University Press.

Scott, P. (1999) View from here, *The Independent: Education,* 11 March.

Shattock, M. (1998) Dearing on governance – the wrong prescription, *Higher Education Quarterly*, 52(1): 35–47.

Shirley, R. (1983) Identifying the levels of strategy for a college or university, *Long Range Planning*, 16(3): 92–8.

Sizer, J. (1982) Assessing institutional performance and progress, in L. Wagner (ed.) *Agenda for Institutional Change*. Guildford: Society for Research into Higher Education.

Smith, D. (1998) Crossing the public–private divide, *Management Today*, August: 26–30.

Smith, D., Scott, P., Bocock, J. and Bargh, C. (1999) Vice-Chancellors and executive leadership in UK Universities: new roles and relationships? in M. Henkel and B. Little (eds) *Changing Relationships Between Higher Education and the State*. London: Jessica Kingsley.

Swain, H. (1999) Staff fear call to log their love interests, *Times Higher Education Supplement*, 29 January: 3.

Tarplett, P. and Parston, G. (1998) *Managing Strategy: A Management Workbook*. London: Office for Public Management.

Taylor, P. (1999) *Making Sense of Academic Life: Academics, Universities and Change*. Buckingham: SRHE and Open University Press.

Thomas, H. (1996) Strategic planning, in D. Warner and D. Palfreyman (eds) *Higher Education Management: The Key Elements*. Buckingham: SRHE and Open University Press.

Thompson, E.P. (ed.) (1970) *Warwick University Ltd. Industry, Management and the Universities*. Middlesex: Penguin Books.

Thorley, H. (ed.) (1998) *Take a Minute: Reflections on Modern Higher Education Administration*. Lancaster: Lancaster University Innovation in Higher Education Series.

Thurow, L. (1972) Education and economic inequality, *Public Interest*, 28: 68–81.

Times Higher Education Supplement (1998) A taste for tribunals, 30 October: 6.

Trapp, R. (1998) What makes a good boss? *Independent on Sunday*, 6 September: 1.

Trowler, P.R. (1998a) *Academics Responding to Change: New Higher Education Frameworks and Academic Cultures.* Buckingham: SRHE and Open University Press.

Trowler, P.R. (1998b) *Education Policy: A Policy Sociology Approach.* Eastbourne: Gildredge Press.

Tysome, T. (1997) Leyland bows out after calls for resignation, *Times Higher Education Supplement*, 4 July: 3.

Tysome, T. (1999) Clever is as clever does, *Times Higher Education Supplement*, 14 May: 22–3.

United Nations Educational, Scientific and Cultural Organization (UNESCO) (1998) *Draft World Declaration on Higher Education for the Twenty-first Century: Vision and Action.* 9 October. Paris: UNESCO.

University of Brighton (1995) University governance. Board of Governors paper B/50/97.

University of Brighton (1999) Report from the part-time provision working group. Academic Development Committee paper ADC/3/99.

Utley, A. (1998) . . . and the academics who feel betrayed, *Times Higher Education Supplement,* 25 September: 5.

Watson, D. (1995) Quality assessment and self-regulation; the English experience, 1992–94, *Higher Education Quarterly*, 49(4): 326–40.

Watson, D. (1998) The limits to diversity, in D. Jary and M. Parker (eds) *The New Higher Education: Issues and Directions for the Post-Dearing University.* Staffordshire: Staffordshire University Press.

Watson, D. (1999) Decoding Dearing on diversity, in M. Henkel and B. Little (eds) *Changing Relationships Between Higher Education and the State.* London: Jessica Kingsley.

Watson, D. and Bowden, R. (1999) Why did they do it?: The Conservative government and mass higher education, 1979–97, *Journal of Education Policy*, 14(3): 243–56.

Watson, D. and Taylor, R. (1998) *Lifelong Learning and the University: A Post-Dearing Agenda.* London: Falmer Press.

Whittington, R. (1993) *What is Strategy – And Does it Matter?* London and Boston: International Thompson Business Press.

Williams, G. (1997) The market route to mass higher education: British experience 1979–1996, *Higher Education Policy*, 10(3/4): 275–89.

Womack, P. (1999) Ac-cen-tchuate the Positive, *Council for College and University English News*, 10 (Winter 1999): 3–5.

Wragg, E. (1997) View from here, *Independent: Education*, 3 April.

Zellick, G. (1994) *Student Disciplinary Procedures: Notes of Guidance.* London: CVCP.

INDEX